LIVING AT THE TOP

HOW TO PROSPER GOD'S WAY AND AVOID THE PITFALLS OF SUCCESS

Jesse Duplantis

Tulsa, Oklahoma

LIVING AT THE TOP
How to Prosper God's Way and
Avoid the Pitfalls of Success
Copyright © 2016 by Jesse Duplantis
ISBN: 978-168031-094-8

Published by Harrison House Publishers
P.O. Box 35035
Tulsa, Oklahoma 74153
www.harrisonhouse.com

Table of Contents

CHAPTER 1

~

Living at the TOP!
Accepting God's Blessing System and
Letting Go of the Status Quo

Over 20 years ago, I was waiting in a greenroom with John Osteen, Joel's father, to be called out for a guest appearance on TBN. We were just chatting about faith and what it meant to live "in the blessing" of God. There were a few people in the room helping us to prepare to go on air—helping us put on microphones, touching up the makeup for TV, and things like that—when suddenly John Osteen said something that has stuck with me for years.

"I live off the *top* of the barrel," John said. Now, being from an oil-producing state like Louisiana, I immediately understood and agreed with his analogy as it related to faith in God for provision. But, I could see a few others in the room didn't agree and just as I was about to say something to add to the conversation about faith, one of the network's staff members asked John a question.

"Well, that's *not* faith is it, Brother Osteen?" she said.

I love what John said next. "Let me tell you something. It took a lot of faith to *fill* that barrel and it takes a lot of faith to *keep* that barrel full."

I've never forgotten that statement. It began to percolate in me that day and, in this book, I hope to reveal how you can live the same way. I pray you will be inspired to stop some of the thought patterns and behaviors that hinder you from being where you really want to be in life—AT THE TOP!

Whatever area you want to focus upon, God's Word has principles that can help you to achieve the top-level-living that you desire. No more barely getting by. No more bottom-of-the-barrel thinking. Whether it's in your finances, your relationships, thoughts in your mind, or the desires in your heart—God has a richer, fuller, and more rewarding life in store for you if you live by the principles in His Holy Word.

It's time to rise up, shake off the old ways, and make a quality decision to do whatever it takes to be where God wants you to be in life. C'mon, you can do it! God will be with you every step of the way. I pray this book helps you to take giant steps towards your rightful place in life—and I believe with all my heart that God not only *can* but *will* show Himself strong through *you*.

I pray that one day you will look back, as John did and as I do today, and see that your "barrel" never once ran dry and in fact, God filled your life to a state of "overflow" once you learned and applied His wonderful principles for *Living at the TOP!*

"And the Lord shall make thee <u>the head, and not the</u> <u>tail</u>; and thou shalt be <u>above only, and thou shalt not be</u> <u>beneath</u>; if that thou hearken unto the commandments of the Lord thy God, which I command thee this day, <u>to observe and to do them.</u>"

Deuteronomy 28:13, emphasis mine

YOU HAVE A CHOICE: THE BLESSING SYSTEM OR THE BABYLONIAN SYSTEM

Is there another way? This is a vitally important question. There's been so much wrong theology concerning the blessing of the Lord—and the sad truth is that both the "church world" and the "secular world" really have accepted the same system when it comes to finances. What system? The Babylonian system.

The Babylonian system is debt-driven. For most people, the mindset for getting ahead in terms of things can pretty much be boiled down to one question: "How much is the note?" That might sound funny, but it's true. Nobody cares about the final cost of anything unless they can swing the monthly note—even churches end up living this way.

Why do people do it? I believe because they think there is no other way to get what they need or want. In fact, the whole world seems to constantly reinforce the notion that ever-increasing debt is normal and necessary. The unspoken rule is that there is no other way except the Babylonian way.

Of course, there is another way, another "system" so to speak—and I like to call it "The Blessing System." In the very first chapter in the very first book of the Bible, the instructions on how to live under God's system of blessing are given.

"And God blessed them, and God said unto them, Be fruitful, and multiply, and replenish the earth, and subdue it: and have dominion over the fish of the sea, and over the fowl of the air, and over every living thing that moveth upon the earth."

Genesis 1:28

So, what are the main four commandments from God to man about living on this earth? Let's look at them and boil it down to what's simple and doable.

1) **BE FRUITFUL**—always producing.

2) **MULTIPLY**—always increasing.

3) **REPLENISH**—always fill and refill. In other words, yes, you are meant to use and consume, but you are also obligated by God to restock, refill, and replace what you've used.

4) **SUBDUE**—control your environment. If you don't control your environment, your environment will control you. In other words, things will come up in life that need to be subdued and put back into the rightful order.

Do you want to live off the top of the barrel instead of drowning at the bottom? Do you want to live at the top in life or scrape the bottom? Then, you must see these basic principles as important for success. Each commandment from God matters, whether you like it or not—and attending to each one of them is what will develop the mindset and the behavior patterns that will lead to success.

You cannot do just one. The principles are each meant to be used during your life. At various times one may seem to be more needful than the others, but expect to use every single one—be fruitful, multiply, replenish, and subdue.

It wouldn't be a bad idea to keep these four words somewhere you can see them each day—either written or typed—to remind yourself that, in all things, if you are aiming for God's best, you will have opportunities at every juncture to be fruitful, multiply, replenish, and subdue. If you can recognize those opportunities, God will lead you to do what you need to do, and you will always be on the right track to succeeding God's way.

GOD DIDN'T CREATE YOU TO BE STAGNANT, HE CREATED YOU TO LEARN AND GROW

Now, the blessing system has nothing to do with your background, culture, or the color of your skin. The only reason people assume it does is because they have the wrong mindset. They've just accepted the wrong system, and might not have even noticed.

But just because you've thought one way your whole life does not mean you have to *keep* thinking or living that way. All human beings are capable of growing and making changes—in fact, all of us are changing every day, like it or not.

Whenever you feel you're in a rut or stuck in life, take that as your soul's signal that you are in need of growth in God, and your mind is crying out to be pushed forward in life—because you were created to grow.

Most people are happiest when they are growing as individuals—moving forward and having not only something to look forward to but the active daily enjoyment of growing as a person. Stagnation is like a miniature form of death for the soul. Stagnating in life isn't what God wants for us.

God did not create us to stay in one place day-after-day in our minds. He wants us to strive for His understanding and His wisdom. However, we can't do that until we notice that we are stuck and begin making changes in the way that we think. We must stop believing the lies that keep us living lower than we should.

FAITH IN GOD IS AGAINST THE POVERTY MINDSET

John 10:10 is a familiar scripture that says Jesus came to give us *life*, and *life more abundantly*. So, Jesus did not push a "barely-getting-by" mindset—don't let religious people fool you. But He definitely pushed a "life more abundantly" mindset. Jesus consistently preached about the limitless love of God for the world and His children, the all-powerful nature of God, and the power of faith in the life of the true believer.

Many very good people I meet love God, but they've simply accepted the poverty mentality of the world—the Babylonian system—as if they are the children of a barely-getting-by God, instead of a limitless one Who is solely moved by our faith.

Whether it comes to finances, relationships, abilities, or the state of mind we inhabit, most Christians don't expect anything much higher than the status quo in life. Sure, they might *wish* for better, but they don't really believe their life will actually *get* any better—therefore it doesn't.

Nothing much comes from wishing except that it stretches your imagination, but there is always a tinge of doubt attached to wishing. Hope is a much better alternative because hope is the first step to faith, and faith is what not only pleases God, but actually changes things.

Faith in God is at odds with the poverty mindset for this simple reason—God is not impoverished and we are called to be imitators of Him, as dear children. Consider Heaven. Consider the very earth you live on. Neither could be considered poverty-stricken. People do all sorts of things to bring poverty and harm to others in this world, but the earth itself is abundant and filled with provision for all of mankind.

It's a Lie—There Is Nothing Holy About Lack

Of course, the "poverty mindset" goes way beyond finances, but finances are the easiest to relate it to, so let's look at that for a moment. Some religions go so far as to take a "holy vow of poverty" in an effort to shed themselves of material things and serve God and their church in a better way.

How anyone can call poverty "holy" is beyond me. After all, which is better: 1) to have something to enjoy and give, or 2) have nothing to enjoy and give? In my opinion, it's selfish to deliberately choose poverty—it's *not* holy.

Holiness is a reverence to God and His ways, and one of the many things the Bible teaches over and over is that we should use our gifts and talents, be a conduit of the Holy Spirit in the earth, and live a generous life of giving.

When a baby is starving to death and dying, is it good and holy? When you get thrown out of your home because you can't pay the mortgage note, is it good and holy? When a family is so in debt that they end up borrowing even more just to pay back what they already owe at 20-30%, is that good and holy? When a person has the ability to be a blessing to others, but chooses not to, is that good and holy? No, of course not, is the answer to all those questions. Poverty is not a blessing to anyone. Poverty is a curse.

CREDIT CARD COMPANIES WILL TAKE ADVANTAGE OF WHATEVER WE WILL ACCEPT

Today, companies are taking more and more advantage of people who have fallen into the Babylonian mindset. Mafia guys have gone to prison for loan-sharking and yet, many credit card companies practically do the same thing, and the whole world just goes along with it—falling deeper and deeper into the hole. That poverty mentality is something creditors take advantage of and it's just ridiculous.

At one time, credit cards had interest rates that were much, much lower. The only reason they have the nerve to keep upping the interest rate is because we all just keep accepting it. They know that they can charge nearly any amount of interest that they want to charge—because we have shown them that we will accept it if the monthly note is low enough. That's how bad we want what we want. That's how much we believe that there is no other way.

At the time that I'm writing this book, gasoline has been hovering for over 1,000 days at over $3 a gallon in the United States—and now we are so accustomed to it that nobody complains as much anymore. If it drops two pennies, in fact, people get excited. Why? We've accepted the higher cost as "normal" and so what once was just crazy is now a part of daily life.

MAKE A CHOICE NOT TO ACCEPT THE RELIGIOUS STATUS QUO

This book, of course, is not about oil prices or even debt—but it is about what we grow to *accept* in our own mind and in our own life. If we want to live at the top in life, we must make a choice NOT to accept the status quo. We have to challenge the old way we've been thinking in order to accept a new way of thinking.

You leave the Babylonian system in your mind first. You learn to look with new eyes and you decide that you don't *want* to live the world's way anymore. So, you make a choice *not* to keep doing things the same way you've always done them.

I pray this book helps you to adopt a new way of thinking—one that includes greater faith in God and a fresh look at His Word as it applies to prosperity. I have also included some teaching on how you can avoid the pitfalls of success that have derailed the lives of so many people throughout the ages. The more you know, the easier it will be to believe God for big things and sidestep the common heart issues that crop up in yourself and others as you make your way to the top!

God loves you—and His Word works! He has so much more for you than you can even imagine! *"Now unto Him that is able to do exceeding abundantly above all that we ask or think, according to the power that worketh in us, Unto Him be glory in the church by Christ Jesus throughout all ages, world without end. Amen"* (Ephesians 3:20-21).

CHAPTER 2

You Have the Same Faith as Abraham and He Was "Very Rich!"

Most people ask me about wealth—either to find out what God has to say about it or to fight me for believing certain verses. People are interested in money because it's a form of power in the earth. You need it to live in this economic world and the more you have, the more you can do and give to help others—it's as simple as that.

The Old Testament talks a lot about wealth, and it tells you both the good and bad side of being financially successful. Of course, there are always two sides to every story. If you have the wrong heart about wealth or use it to do the wrong things, of course, the outcome will not be very good.

Any homiletical, hermeneutical, philosophical, or theological teaching that's taken to the extreme can go off-course if a person has the wrong motive or actions. If that's the case, whatever began as a blessing can eventually turn into what feels like a curse in your life.

ABRAHAM IS YOUR SPIRITUAL ANCESTOR
LEARN FROM HIS SUCCESSES AND FAILURES

Abraham is called the father of faith in the Scripture and we, as believers, have been adopted into his family of faith. You are the "seed of Abraham." I am the seed of Abraham. According to the Word, all children of God are the seed of Abraham. That makes Abraham *your* ancestor. Think about that.

Take ownership of your position in the family of faith. Remember that God had a great plan for Abraham's life, but it was only because Abraham *chose to believe* God's plan that he gained his rightful title as "the father of faith."

The title wasn't just given to him. He earned it. What was the *currency* that God established as valid in order for Abraham to not only earn the title, but also to receive the blessings God promised to him? It was comprised of just two things: *Belief* and *obedience*—the same two things God considers valid today, too.

Let's learn from our spiritual ancestor of faith because he was just a man like you and me, and he had both great successes and a few failures. Let's learn from him now. First, here is the promise God made to Abraham:

> *"Now the LORD had said unto Abram, Get thee out of thy country, and from thy kindred, and from thy father's house, unto a land that I will shew thee:*
> *"And I will make of thee a great nation, and <u>I will bless thee</u>, and make thy name great; and <u>thou shalt be a blessing</u>:*

"And I will bless them that bless thee, and curse him that curseth thee: and in thee shall all families of the earth be blessed."

Genesis 12:1-3, emphasis mine

Abraham's New Way of Believing God

Abraham believed what God said. In fact, He believed it so much that Abraham began to do something that nobody had been recorded as having done before—it was revolutionary and it was a God-kind of thing. Abraham began to speak *as if* the promise had already come to pass. He spoke like it had happened *before* it happened. This strange new way of thinking and speaking is what gave Abraham an edge like no other man before him. His heart and mind was in unity with the promise.

Abraham was acting like the God of creation Who *spoke* and things came to pass. Go and look at Genesis and you will see that this is how the Word tells us that God brought things into existence— He started with words.

Abraham's new way of believing God's words is what actually *caused* God's words to come to pass. His faith drew it in to fruition. You see, when Abraham *believed* enough to *speak as if it had already come to pass,* Abraham was showing that he thought the promises of God were so solid and so secure that it was just a matter of time before he saw them physically. Abraham believed that God was trustworthy.

FAITH IS FAITH: THIS IS WHAT'S INSIDE OF YOU

Now, look at some of the verses in the New Testament that describe Abraham's faith. As you read, remember that this man is YOUR ancestor—what he had inside of him long ago is exactly what you have inside of you today.

> *"Therefore it is of faith, that it might be by grace; to the end the promise might be sure to all the seed; not to that only which is of the law, but to that also which is of **the faith of Abraham; who is the father of us all,***
>
> *"(As it is written, I have made thee a father of many nations,) before him whom he believed, even God, who quickeneth the dead, and **calleth those things which be not as though they were.***
>
> *"Who against hope **believed in hope**, that he might become the father of many nations, according to that which was spoken, **So shall thy seed be.***
>
> *"And being **not weak in faith**, he **considered not his own body** now dead, when he was about an hundred years old, neither yet the deadness of Sarah's womb:*
>
> *"**He staggered not at the promise of God through unbelief; but was strong in faith, giving glory to God;***
>
> *"And **being fully persuaded that, what He had promised, He was able also to perform.***
>
> *"And therefore it was imputed to him for righteousness.*

"Now it was not written for his sake alone, that it was imputed to him;

"But for us also, to whom it shall be imputed, if we believe on him that raised up Jesus our Lord from the dead;

"Who was delivered for our offences, and was raised again for our justification."

Romans 4:16-25, emphasis mine

Again, do you realize that the same faith that Abraham had is the <u>same faith</u> that you've been given? Think about it. God doesn't give one type of faith to one person and a different type of faith to another person—faith is faith.

"We having the <u>same spirit of faith</u>, according as it is written, I believed, and therefore have I spoken; we also believe, and therefore speak."

2 Corinthians 4:13, emphasis mine

Accept it—you have the *same* faith as Abraham, the father of faith. Say it to yourself. Acknowledge that you have no more and no less. Now, what are you going to do with it?

What You Hear *Repetitively* Matters

If you want to live at the top, you should focus on strengthening or growing your faith. You grow the "mustard seed" within you only one way: "By hearing and hearing by the Word of God" (Romans 10:17).

Notice that the scripture says both "hearing" and "hearing by the Word of God." This tells us that whatever we hear over and over will grow our faith in what we are hearing. Again, what we hear repetitively *matters.*

Wherever you point yourself in your mind and heart is exactly where your feet will end up taking you. To grow our faith in God and have true success, we must repetitively hear what matters in everyday life—the *Word* of God. The Scripture is alive and powerful because what was inspired and spoken by God has an energy force within it unlike natural words. This means it's not just a bunch of old stories—it's life-giving principles that can help you both daily and as you reach for long-term goals in life.

The Word has both direct instruction and stories and both are there to help you live a better life. Stories illustrate points that reveal God, His power, and our human nature in relation to Him and natural circumstances. *All* scripture is given by God for instruction in righteousness (2 Timothy 3:16).

Even the stories are there to teach us. We see where people went right and where people went wrong, and it's often the very same people doing the right thing one minute and missing it the next! Let that give you hope that you can make the right choices and be spirit-led to a life of goodness and success God's way. You have more information than they did at the time and yet, even if you mess up, God will help you to get back on the right track if you turn to Him.

Garbage in, garbage out—it's what goes into your mind that matters because your life follows your thoughts and words.

The concepts in the Word will totally change your success rate in life if you repetitively hear them and apply them. So, make God's Word a priority. It matters.

If you want to live at the top, you have to focus on where you are going and give yourself tools for the journey—the Word is a life-changing tool for success. Remember, the seed of faith itself is already in you. The Word will "water" that seed. What's good must be focused on more than what isn't. Create a path for your own success by "hearing and hearing by the Word of God."

God may lead you to do some hard things. Remember that God is good and anything He asks of you is intended to stretch you and take you to a higher place in His plan for your life.

CHAPTER 3

◦⸒

If You Want to Live at the Top, You Will Need to Subdue Fear

Obedience is better than sacrifice—and the story of Abraham's life illustrates this point well. After God told Abraham to leave Egypt the Bible says, *"And Abram went out of Egypt, he, and his wife, and all that he had, **and Lot with him,** into the south"* (Genesis 13:1, emphasis mine).

Now, remember that only one chapter before, in Genesis 12:1, God told Abraham not only to *"get thee out of thy country"* but also to get away *"from thy kindred."* Why would he disobey and take Lot with him when God expressly told him to go away from his kin? One reason. Fear.

Abraham is called the father of faith, but he didn't do everything right. In fact, he had moments of doubt and disobedience like all of us. The Bible records them to show us the trouble we end up in when we lose sight of our faith in God's Word and instead live by our own fears. God had a huge world-changing plan for Abraham and his wife, Sarah. It was beyond what they could do on their own.

If you want to live at the top, one thing you must realize is that fear is a natural part of the human mind, but it is something you must subdue if you want God's best in your life. Use your faith in God to conquer your fear of walking out His plan.

Let Not Your Heart Be Troubled, Neither Let It Be Afraid

Remember that doing something new can make you feel apprehensive. Doing something God has said will cause your mind to tilt! This is why to live life at the top, you can't fall into the trap of worry. If you want to succeed, you can't allow your mind to take you for a ride—fear must be dealt with. Subdue it! Do it with the Word of God.

For every fear that comes up to your mind, replace it with the Word of God. Talk to yourself if you have to. Remind yourself aloud of what God has said. Tell your mind to shut up. If you wait until you "feel" like doing what God said, you may never do it—so don't wait to subdue fear when you feel like it. Do it. Move forward and stop looking back.

Let not your heart be troubled. Neither *let* it be afraid. You can *let* fear take you for a ride or you can stop it from taking you for a ride— you have power and you have choice.

What God has spoken, He will *make* good. Notice that God didn't ask Abraham to "perform" the promise. He won't ask you to either. God just asks us to *believe* what He said and *obey* His Word. Again, obedience is better than sacrifice.

You see, it doesn't matter what you give up for God—if He didn't ask you to do it, it's just a waste of time. All He wants is somebody who will believe Him, do what He said, and have the "life" that Jesus came to give "more abundantly." That's it. It's all good! But it's hard to move forward into unknown territory because the human mind likes comfort and complacency. The human mind tries to protect us sometimes from the adventures of faith. It likes to keep us in survival mode, but God has no fear of your future and He doesn't want your mind riddled with worry, anxiety, or little fears that cut you off from His wonderful plan for your life.

DON'T SECOND-GUESS THE GOD OF THE UNIVERSE

Would you second-guess the God of the universe? Abraham did. The problem wasn't that he didn't have faith in God; after all, he listened to God and left Egypt. The problem was that he didn't subdue the "little" fears inside of him that, for whatever reason, caused him to directly disobey God by bringing his nephew, Lot, along with him.

In fact, Abraham had a few times in his life when fear brought him a lot of trouble and changed the course of his life—and our world, even—forever. This is what happens when you disobey God and make choices based in fear instead of faith.

If you let it, fear will try to run your life and change your course. Instead of God being in control, your fear will be in control. It'll be a much harder path to where God is calling you to be—at the top.

Fear can make you stop doing what you're meant to do, which is have faith in God and live at peace as you move forward in whatever He's asked you to do or you're believing for. Fear can also compel you to do things you *don't* really want to do; it can get you so sidetracked in your own mind that you spin and make bad choices because you can't focus on your vision.

Why did Abraham think he needed his nephew so badly that he disobeyed God and took him along? Well, you must remember what God said to Abraham. "I'll make you the father of many nations...," and you must remember that Abraham's wife, Sarah, was barren. She had never had a child. She didn't seem to be able to become pregnant and she was very old.

Sarah was beautiful. In fact, Abraham had a wife that was so stunning that the Word says a king desired to have her when she was 80 years old. Think about that. Now, you've got to be one fine looking woman to have something like that happen! Abraham loved her but he knew that to become "the father of many nations," as God had said to him, Sarah would need a miracle.

So, what do you think happens in the mind of a man with that kind of vision who is leaving home at a late age in life with a barren wife? Do you think his mind was just going to accept God's Word? Or, do you think his mind would fight him and use fear to make him alter the plan ever so slightly? You got it! Fear came. It always does. Now that you know this, you don't have to be caught unaware when it strikes you too—because it will. Subdue it!

Abraham likely thought something like, *Well, in the natural it doesn't look like I'm ever going to have children. I know God said it, but I don't know how it's going to happen. What if I die on the way? What if it doesn't happen like God said? What if I misunderstood Him? I can't just let all my possessions go. I need a successor. I'll take one person, my nephew, Lot....just in case.*

Now, this sounds like good sense talking—and it would be total common sense to do this IF God hadn't expressly told Abraham to get away from his family. He was supposed to go out with only Sarah. That was God's plan. He got scared. This is what happens when fear gets involved and instead of obeying, a contingency plan is made in case God doesn't come through. That's doubt working and it's not to your advantage to let fear take you for a ride. Put it down.

You Can't Go God's Way
If You're Pointing Yourself the Other Way

The problem with Lot was that he had an eye for the world, and not an eye for God. The Bible said he *"pitched his tent toward*

Sodom because the grass was green." It's such an interesting picture the Bible paints here and there are more than a couple points that could be made here. I'll just say this. The greener the grass, the greater the deception! Where you pitch your tent *toward* is where you mentally really want to go, and whether you go or not is not really the issue—your mind is already there.

> **You cannot go God's way if you are pointing
> yourself in the opposite direction.
> Pitch your tent towards godly success—
> and not towards Sodom.**

What you repetitively hear changes you. What you repetitively look at changes you. Your mind works this way. It's how God created you. *"As a man thinketh, so is he"* (Proverbs 23:70).

Losing focus on what God wants for you is easy; just focus on something else. You will end up second-guessing everything, rehashing every fear and doubt, and either living from chaos to chaos or doing nothing much. It's called double-mindedness, according to the Word, and it'll throw you to and fro like a rudderless ship (James 1:8).

If you think Abraham didn't do the right thing when it came to taking his nephew, Lot—and I'll come back to him in a moment—just look at what happened between Abraham and his wife, Sarah.

Fear Wrestles with the "How's" and "Why's"

Again, remember, Sarah was a childless woman. There was no medical help available at the time to help her conceive. The Bible doesn't tell us what was exactly wrong inside her body, we just know that she was in her 80's and had never had a baby.

We can imagine that Sarah's heart was struck with fear when she heard what God had told her husband—how can an old woman be a part of her husband's vision of being "a father of many nations" when she has been barren from the time she was a young woman?

Faith takes God at His Word. Fear wrestles with the "how's" and "why's" to the point of mental exhaustion.

Fear causes people to make poor choices. Sarah had such fear about her own body and such worry about God's ability to do what He said for Abraham, that she literally told her husband to have sex with her maid. She wanted her husband to have what God said so much and she was so riddled with fear that she couldn't make it happen that she literally pushed him into the tent of another woman. Now, most men would think they hit the lottery if their wife gave them full permission to have sex with another woman! The Bible never records Abraham arguing with Sarah about it even though, of course, he knew it was wrong. He just did what he was told! I can almost hear him saying, "Okay, Sarah, I'm gonna do this, but only for your sake."

Abraham didn't subdue his own fear. He didn't help his wife to subdue her fear either; he could have, but he didn't. Instead, he let her fear drive him right into Hagar's tent.

There Are Always Consequences to Bad Choices

Abraham and the maid, Hagar, had a baby. So, you could say that Sarah was actually the first surrogate mother and it didn't work out for the family. Ishmael was born. And, just a few years later, Sarah came up pregnant—a true miracle that made her laugh, which is why Isaac was named Isaac, which means "laughter." Trouble ensued.

It was a tense situation with them all living together, and Sarah was angry about how Ishmael was treating Isaac. After so many years of being childless, she was very protective of her only child and when she heard Ishmael making fun of Isaac, she lost it. She asked Abraham to force Hagar and Ishmael out of the camp, and he did. This began the Arab-Israeli problem the world still deals with today.

It hurt Abraham to watch Hagar and their son leave the camp because he loved them, and he prayed to God for them to survive. God honored Abraham, the Word says, and told him that his son, Ishmael, would not only survive, but that his descendents would prosper and be like the sands of the earth in that, there would be so many.

> **God warned us though that, in character,
> Ishmael's seed would be wild— as wild as a "bunch
> of wild asses." It sounds harsh, but remember that
> *God* didn't create the situation.
> *Fear* created the situation.**

We were created as free-will beings and God won't force us to submit to His will. Sarah made a choice not to subdue her fear. Abraham saw his distraught wife and didn't help her to subdue it either. They went along with it instead of tackling the root problem, which was fear of not having what God said they could have.

Abraham made a fear-based choice and Hagar didn't have much she could do about it; the culture dictated that she listen and obey. So, it isn't really about fault. It's about what happens when fear motivates people.

God didn't create Ishmael's lineage to be this way. God simply prophesied how it was all going to turn out. God promised that even though it was not His plan for Abraham to sleep with the maid, He would make sure that Ishmael was protected from death and that he would not only live but his seed would multiply greatly.

> **Never forget that while there is grace and mercy
> from God for any poor choice—forgiveness and a
> way to come back into His original plan—there are
> *always* consequences to every action.**

The ripple effect can be staggering because for every giant plan of God, there will always be an attack coming. Don't forget that there is an enemy of God and man.

The Ripple Effects of a Fear-Based Choice

It couldn't have been easy for Ishmael to grow up knowing that that he was the son of Abraham, a great man of faith in God, but also born out of Abraham's moment of weakness. Weakness not just towards his wife, but in patience with God's plan. This weakness created a domino effect, which caused him to reject his son in order to keep the peace with his wife.

Perhaps this ancient rejection is the root cause for some of the modern day problems we see in the Middle Eastern world today. This desire by the sons of Ishmael to displace the sons of Isaac could be a way to get back at an ancient father. You see, unforgiveness, misunderstanding, hurt, anger, and hatred can all be passed down through the generations.

Now, God's promise to Abraham and Sarah still came true in their lives and their son, Isaac, took his rightful place in God's original plan. However, the fear-motivated choice to sleep with Hagar to produce offspring because God's plan wasn't going quickly enough for them had a trickle down effect. I believe that a lot of the Middle Eastern issues between Isaac's sons and Ishmael's sons come from a passed-down ancient root of rejection and until forgiveness flows and both sides are reconciled to their true Father, not Abraham, but God Himself, nothing can be resolved.

How does that apply to your own life here and now? Well, we are all the sons and daughters of our own forefathers, but it is our job to notice that we can change whatever has been passed down to us. We aren't hopeless and the ripple effect can be stopped with you. It's within all of our ability to step back and recognize when we are just following a tradition of hurt.

No matter what has happened in the past, we don't have to become what our fathers became and we don't have to look through the lens of anger. If wrong was done, we can forgive, release, and make things right. God is love. He lives within us and He is fully able to help us overcome past hurts no matter how many generations deep they run.

There are so many points that can be made and learned from both Abraham's successes and failures in his faith in God, but the one I want to make right now is this: Don't complicate your life and your children's lives by taking matters into your own hands. If God has told you to trust Him with a situation that seems hopeless, trust Him. Be patient! You are going to live forever, eternally, and this life is but a vapor. Don't let the devil trick you into thinking this life is long and your time waiting in patience is an insurmountable struggle. It's not your job to "fix" God's promise to fit your timeline. It's your job to simply *believe* and *act* on that belief.

If You Want to Live at the Top, Fear Must Be Subdued

The choices we make matter, and fear must be subdued. If we want to live at the top, fear cannot be allowed to dictate our choices in life. The Bible says in 1 John 4:18 that *"perfect love casteth out all fear,"* so whenever you find yourself falling prey to fears or worries, you can bet that you need to pay attention to your mindset when it comes to love. Love and fear are connected, but they are just at the opposite ends of the spectrum.

There is no perfect love except the love of God. Do you believe that He loves you? Everyone will say they believe that, but their faith doesn't always show it. So, let me ask you a few things. Do you believe God loves you enough to honor His Word to you? Do you think perhaps you've done the unthinkable and there is less love for you than needed to receive His promises? Many people cling to guilt and a low feeling of unworthiness for the blessings of God. If you do that, you have to settle it in your heart that God can't lie.

You might think, "Well, I know that! I know God can't lie." Do you really? Because when you know that God can't lie, then you believe the truth that Jesus has redeemed you, that He washed away your sin on the cross over 2,000 years ago. The cross isn't just a nice story. It's the dividing line between life and death for everyone. It's what made it possible for you to know God, and not just know about God. The death and resurrection of Jesus Christ paid the price for you. All your sin. All your iniquity. All your guilt and shame. What does "all" mean? It means ALL!

So, did God lie when He sent His Son to die for your sin? Did He lie? You need to look through the eyes of the blood to really see what God sees when He looks at YOU, because you are clean and washed as white as snow in the precious blood of Jesus. Don't make that a small thing in your mind. That is how much God loves you.

> **Do you secretly think you don't deserve God's promises or a truly good life? Do you think things will always go badly? If so, then you don't understand love—and you need to focus on God's love for you.**

Focus on getting wisdom and getting understanding when it comes to God's love for you. Then, as you stretch your faith to meet His promises, just notice where your mind goes when you think of success and what it means for you personally to "live at the top." If you feel a hesitancy about godly success in any area—spiritually, physically, financially, in relationships, etc.—you need to know this. Fear is trying to hijack your future.

Thoughts rooted in fear are not rooted in the love of God. If we want to live at the top, subduing fear and focusing on the love that God has towards us is paramount because how can we have faith in Someone in whom we don't really believe? How can we trust if we don't *know* He loves us? We can't. You can't look forward if you are continually looking back. Think about it. Subdue fear!

SUBDUE FEAR WITH LOVE
THE WORD IS LOVE IN WRITTEN FORM

So, how do you subdue and combat inner fear? With love—and the Word of God is love in written form. Just reading what God has done for you, what He thinks about you, and what He wants for you will grow the faith within you. God literally is love. He is pure, good, and righteous and every promise in His Word is rooted in knowing His love. To rely on His love if you are dealing with fear, use the Word of God and put yourself in the verses.

You can't fight fearful thoughts totally on your own. To truly succeed at a deep level, your mouth needs to *say* the Word so that your own ears *hear* the Word. You believe what you say more than anybody, so start saying good things. Speak the Word over yourself. Don't dismiss this.

I don't care if you have to stand in front of a mirror in your room and look yourself right in the eye and talk to yourself in order to stir up your faith—do it. This is a discipline that will change your life. For example, you could put yourself in 1 John 4:19 and say, "I love you, God, because You first loved me."

Take claim of John 3:16-17 and say, "You sent Your only begotten Son, Jesus, to this earth out of Your love for me! I believed on Jesus and I'll never perish—I have everlasting life because of Your love. You did not send Jesus to condemn me, but to save me and thank You for that!"

Insert yourself in Romans 5:5, "Thank You for the gift of the Holy Spirit, Who has poured out Your great love into my heart." Claim the words of 2 Timothy 1:7, "I have not been given a spirit of fear but of love, power, and a sound mind!"

Look up verses or get yourself a quick reference book or file with verses by topic handy, then focus on a few that speak to your heart and put yourself into them every single day. Making the scriptures your own in this way is called "confession" in some circles, but no matter what you call it, doing this will help you to rise up on the inside. The Word of God is powerful and active; it is a living thing because you can't separate God from His Word. If you let Him, He will change you.

Let His love propel you. Refuse to let fear hijack your rightful place in God, which is always going to be at the top!

CHAPTER 4

～

Tangible Riches from a Fearless God

GOD DOESN'T MIND YOU HAVING POSSESSIONS, AS LONG AS POSSESSIONS DON'T HAVE YOU

People who don't believe in tangible prosperity for godly people need to really pay attention to Genesis 13:2:

> *"Abraham was **very rich** in livestock, in silver, and in gold."*

Wait, how rich was Abraham? VERY rich. How rich? VERY. Did we just read this right? The Bible even tells us what exactly he was rich in: *"...in livestock, in silver, and in gold."* So, Abraham followed God and ended up not just barely making it, but VERY rich. Some people don't like the word rich, but apparently God doesn't have a problem with it. Some people think God doesn't care about your prosperity, but that's just not true.

While some people teach differently, the truth is that God has no problem with your prosperity and poverty is not a marker for holiness. Prosperity is not evil. If it was, Heaven would be an evil place because the truth is that Heaven is flush with prosperity in every single area, including material prosperity. The Scriptures tell us that God's home is adorned with things like pearly gates, gold streets, and the foundation of His wall is made of jasper, sapphire, chalcedony, emerald, sardonyx, sardius, chrysolite, beryl, topaz, chrysoprasus, jacinth, amethyst (Revelation 21:18-20).

> **If you think *prosperity* is not godly
> and inherently evil, who do you think made
> the streets of gold in Heaven? Do you think it was
> the *devil* who blessed Abraham?**

God created gold. God blessed Abraham. Jesus told us exactly what the devil does in John 10:10—and blessing people is just not what the devil does. Jesus described the devil as a "thief" who comes to do three things: to steal, to kill, and to destroy. That's it. Everything he does has one of those motives behind it. Besides, how can he "steal" from you if you don't have anything to take? Let the elevator go to the top!

If God didn't endorse prosperity, Abraham wouldn't have become "very rich" by having faith in God. Never forget Abraham was "very rich" in livestock, very rich in silver, and very rich in gold. Remember, these are not spiritual attributes we are talking about here! Livestock, silver, and gold are tangible possessions.

Of course, you can not be successful God's way unless you are spiritually rich first—faith must come before finance. You become spiritually rich by studying the Word, so that it can get inside of you, and by having faith in God and His words so that you can do His Word and His will. It's about endeavoring to keep your heart open, clean, and moldable to His way of doing things, instead of the world's way of doing things. There is nothing wrong with physical possessions. God doesn't mind you having possessions, as long as possessions don't have you—He must come first. You don't serve money; money serves you and you serve the Lord!

Jesus Called Himself "the Son of Man" He Loved the World and Was Proud to Be Human

The church has often tried to pin Jesus as a poor man, but He didn't even start out poor. He was NOT born in a manger because his family was poor. He was born in a manger because there was no room at the inn. We wouldn't know there was no vacancy if Mary and Joseph hadn't tried to get a room, and they wouldn't try to get a room unless they had the money to pay for it.

Besides, Jesus wasn't born for long before He had three rich guys looking for Him—wise men bringing what? Possessions! Gold, frankincense, and myrrh were gifts of high value.

When Jesus was in the ministry, He had twelve people on His staff. Poor men don't have staff. Some of those men on staff were married and Jesus took care of their wives, too. Some theologians say that Jesus also had 70 part-time workers He sent out, so that's eighty-two people in the Jesus Christ of Nazareth Evangelistic Association. I'm making a joke, but it's really no joke. He had a treasurer who was stealing from the bag and not one of the disciples knew about it. Why have Judas if there was no money? How could he steal if there wasn't a surplus of money?

Even right before His crucifixion, they gambled for His robes—so Jesus' clothes must have been pretty nice because people don't gamble for rags! Think about it. Let the elevator go to the top! Did you ever read about Jesus struggling financially? Why didn't He struggle? Because He was the Son of God? No, the Word tells us that He emptied Himself of His heavenly privileges and in fact, Jesus didn't call Himself the Son of God, but instead He liked to call Himself the Son of Man. He was proud to be human.

IF PROSPERITY IS BAD THEOLOGY, WHAT ARE YOU GOING TO DO WHEN YOU GET TO *HEAVEN*?

What are you going to do when you get to Heaven and there's no poverty? What will you think when you see that everybody is full? When there is no such thing as a shack, a homeless person, or a hungry belly? When there is no such thing as brokenness or lack? When every house you see is considered by Christ to be a "mansion." And where nobody is griping about what someone else has, because everyone is prosperous on a level that has never before been seen on earth? Solomon was poor by comparison to the citizens of Heaven. Think about that.

Why won't there be any persecution of people for their prosperity? Because Satan will be in hell....where the trailers are!

The only one who truly HATES the prosperity of God's people is the devil. He knows that this is an economic world and the more blessed God's people are, the greater influence they have on the whole world.

The devil is interested in discrediting God in any way that he can. If he can convince believers that their economic status should be poverty or barely getting by, he will do it. It is in his best interest to keep believers broken and he will try to undermine the truth about the goodness of God in any way that he can— spiritually, physically, and yes, financially!

I made that trailer joke, but this is a mindset that should not be simply about your house. We must realize the tactics of the devil in trying to make poverty something holy from God, when it is completely the opposite of that. There was no lack in the Garden of Eden before sin entered into the realm of humanity.

Listen, there is nothing wrong with a trailer! Don't feel bad for living in one, if you do. I was raised in trailers all my life.

Did it make me a better or worse person? No! The point is that, there is something better for you if you want it, because God is a good God who cares about His children, but He requires that we listen to Him and not the devil when it comes to how we think and live our lives.

Whether you want to live in the smallest house or the biggest house is irrelevant; prosperity is God's will for you so that you can help establish God's covenant of goodness in the earth. All believers have the responsibility to share what we know and help others to live better than they are living today, spiritually, physically, financially, and in any other way that you can.

God will lead you to help others, but how can you really help them if you are fixated on the wrong notion that being financially blessed is not of God? Do you know what the best thing you can do for a poor person is? Not be poor! The more you have, the more you can give. Start wherever you are but don't glorify lack! Work on making giving and helping others a habit.

Resist the urge to cut down others who are prospering. Check your heart. Resist the urge to glorify any sort of lack or poverty. Realize that poverty is a curse, not a blessing. The Garden of Eden was lush and lacking nothing, until sin came in. Then, working by the sweat of our brow became common. So, God didn't institute lack and misery.

**Giving and helping others pushes back against the
notion that we have to only "take care
of ourselves" to survive. No, God's way,
from the beginning was sowing and reaping.
We were created, even before sin,
to continue the cycle of sowing and reaping.**

Any believer worth his salt knows that it's better to give than
to receive. The Scripture says it but it also feels good to our core
to help others. Why? This is how God created His children to
be. Anything that kills, steals, or destroys others is not of God. I
believe that as believers, we are meant to be distribution houses,
always giving and always receiving, and always giving again.

From the words we speak to the blessings we provide others,
we are created to be joyful and generous givers who don't worry
all the time! We are not meant to be anxious and fretting everything as if there is not enough and never will be enough. This
is fear.

We are meant to say "no" to fear no matter how little or
much we have to give, and to rely upon our faith in God and
our hope in His holy Word. It's exactly this "pushing back"
against the human tendency to worry and instead choosing to
have faith in God that changes our circumstances and our peace
of mind! We are meant to live above and not beneath, joyful
and not miserable. We have been created to live off the top of
the barrel.

WEALTH WITHOUT SORROW ATTACHED TO IT
THIS IS GOD'S KIND OF PROSPERITY

I was born poor. Even as a small child, I remember deciding that I would never be poor as an adult. So, before I knew the Lord, I made a way for myself in music and I made more money than I knew what to do with. I did exactly what I decided to do. I was a sinner and a bad man, but I had money.

I remember getting to a place financially in my early 20's that I didn't have to worry about money at all, and I remember feeling so disappointed once I got to that place financially. You see, I had really grown up believing that if I just had money and if I just had enough of it, I'd be happy. I was wrong.

What I found out was that money is useless when it comes to making people happy or peaceful. It didn't make me happy. Money made me more comfortable while I was miserable! When I went into the ministry years later, I had this old idea in my head from childhood churches that money was evil, so I gave away my money in an attempt to please and serve the Lord. I went right back to the lack of my childhood!

It took me years to find out that I didn't have to prove myself to God by living in lack. It's just not what He ever asked of me. He wanted my heart and my life; money was irrelevant at that point!

Even the rich young ruler wouldn't have been lacking money forever if he gave away his riches because sowing and reaping was still in affect then, and Jesus had a plan for the man's life. Jesus didn't tell everybody to "come, follow Me" like He told that rich young ruler. He really only did that when He was picking disciples. So, I believe that Jesus wanted this man in the ministry with Him.

What I want you to know is that Jesus *didn't* tell everybody He saw to give everything they had away in order to please Him. In fact, He only told this one man! And Jesus wouldn't have done that if the rich young ruler hadn't pressed Him after He already gave him the answer.

Remember that Jesus had already answered the man's question, "What shall I do to inherit eternal life?" This was before the cross, so grace through the blood hadn't entered into things just yet so Jesus gave the rich young ruler his answer, "You know the commandments…" He began to tell him some of them, but the rich young ruler didn't let it go. He contended with Jesus when he said, "But I've done all this since I was young." In other words, "What else should I do?"

Jesus felt love for the man then and *that's* when He told him to give it all away and follow Him. So, notice that, first, Jesus told him to follow God's commandments—in other words, do His will. When the man pressed Him, Jesus looked at him with love and talked directly to the man's root problem while also offering the solution to the problem. "Sell what you have" was tagging the man's heart problem—the rich young ruler trusted in his riches more than God. "Follow me" was giving the rich young ruler the solution. It meant he would have to clear up his heart issue by putting God first. If he conquered that hurdle,

Jesus was willing to take him along as He continued to fulfill God's plan for mankind. The rich young ruler just couldn't do it. He couldn't let go of his possessions. Therefore, he couldn't grow and he couldn't accept Jesus' offer to follow Him in the ministry.

CHAPTER 5

~

The Discomfort of Prosperity, Spotting Growth Points, and Handling Change God's Way

Growth is about change, and change is not comfortable. When a baby begins to walk, he is uncomfortable. When a teenage boy begins to grow into a man, he is often uncomfortable. When a woman has a baby, she is extremely uncomfortable!

Birds leave the nest. Trees let their leaves fall. Crabs outgrow their shell and shed it in order to grow a bigger one. None of these natural changes are comfortable, yet each is necessary for growth. One thing that you must become completely aware of is this—growth *requires* change, and change creates discomfort. This is not a bad thing. It's a growth thing!

This is true with living at the top in prosperity, too. Financial blessings don't stop you from being uncomfortable because as you gain them, you will come to junctures in the road, so to speak, that require you to stretch in order to allow God to propel you to even greater heights. These are opportunities to grow that may not feel good, but they will challenge you and you will move forward to greater blessing if you take the challenges well.

Proverbs 10:22 says the blessing of the Lord makes you *rich* and adds *no sorrow* to the riches. But it *doesn't* say that godly prosperity is a continual state of blissful comfort.

I wish money could provide us blissful comfort, but it can't, even when it comes from the Lord. Adam was blessed, but still was required to tend the Garden. Abraham was blessed, but he was still required to tend the herd. You see, God created us to grow and He loves to see us grow. We are created to have adventures in faith and never be stagnant. Growth is not always comfortable! Let's look at Abraham and Lot again with this in mind.

WHEN PROSPERITY MEETS THE GROWTH POINT

Abraham and his nephew, Lot, co-worked a large amount of land. They had livestock and workers to help them tend the animals. Originally the land was enough for them both. Remember that although God told Abraham originally to leave home and not take any family, he took Lot with him and yet, God's hand of blessing was still on Abraham.

Taking Lot along wasn't God's best plan, but Abraham still had faith in God. He left, after all, and was endeavoring to do right and follow God's Word in faith. So, God's hand of blessing was still upon him.

Now, a portion of the land they worked was near Sodom, and we all know that there was some rotten junk going on in Sodom. But, if you read chapter 13 of Genesis, you'll see that there was also some rotten junk going on between Abraham's workers and Lot's workers. While Sodom was knee-deep in immorality, Abraham and Lot had gotten to a place in their relationship that they were knee-deep in strife. Why?

> **The Bible says Abraham and Lot had become so prosperous in possessions that the land they shared could "no longer support them"—in other words, prosperity brought discomfort.**

They had outgrown not only each other as business partners, but also the very land they worked. They had so many animals and so much blessing that the herdsmen of Lot and the herdsmen of Abraham were fighting.

Now, I believe that Lot was prosperous simply because of his association with Abraham because that's what being near to a man who is blessed by God does for you. It blesses you, too. Who you attach yourself to and who you hang around will affect you for better or for worse. In Lot's case, he benefited by being there even though he was never meant to be there.

So, the herdsmen of Lot and the herdsmen of Abraham were bickering. There was strife in the family business. To gain peace,

Abraham decided that they needed to stop working their flocks together and go their separate ways. This is a point I want you to notice right now. Sometimes, prosperity will force you to change what was once a good thing.

> **Growth will force you, like a crab, to shed your shell of comfort. Sometimes you have to make room for yourself and for even more future prosperity.**

That need for change may be disheartening. Change is uncomfortable, but when the growth point comes, you need to see that discomfort as necessary. What you leave behind is supposed to be left behind; that's just part of growing. Birds leave the nest. Crabs outgrow their shells. Boys become men. Is it wrong for a bird to fly and create a new place for himself? No! Is there something wrong with the crab leaving his shell behind to grow a new one? No. Is there some fault with a boy growing into a man? No. This is the way God intended for it to be. This is growth. It's not comfortable, but it's always necessary.

You see, nothing is static in life and nothing ever stays the same. The sooner you grasp that, the happier you will be with each wonderful moment you have here on earth, even the uncomfortable ones that signal to you, "Hey, it's growth time! Get ready for a bigger shell! Get ready to fly! Get ready for the blessings that come next!"

STICK WITH GOD AND DO THINGS HIS WAY

God makes a way for us to grow that can be peaceful, no matter the situation. His peace is in us and it must flow through us. We can have peace of mind and inner contentment whether we "abase or abound" as Paul said; in other words, all the time, even during growth times.

We must not lose our joy, no matter what. The Word says in Nehemiah 8:10 that the joy of the Lord is our strength. I believe we can have joy, whether we are sleeping on a king-sized mattress in a palace or on a dirt floor in a prison. This kind of peace and this kind of joy is found in our relationship with God, it's found in our faith.

When we don't have faith, we won't have peace. When we don't have faith, we will have a hard time sustaining joy. We may have fleeting happiness maybe, but no real joy. We abide in Christ and He abides in us and that is what gives us the foundation to be able to handle what comes our way. He must be intimately woven into our heart if we are to be sustained during the discomfort of growth.

Remember that the Word says that prosperity destroys a fool, so don't be a fool. It's the wisdom of God that we gain that helps us to not be a fool. We should stick with God and do things His way because we need Him. We need His wisdom to prosper and navigate life with grace. It's that simple!

Scripture warns us to remember and not to forget the Lord when we become prosperous (Deuteronomy 8:18). We must keep God first and in the center of our lives. This is how He not only establishes His covenant on the earth, but also how we open ourselves up for greater and greater wealth and blessing into our lives, again, with no sorrow attached (Proverbs 10:22).

Abraham moved through his growth point with the Lord with grace, honor, and wisdom. Even though he was a "very rich" man, he never trusted in his prosperity or put it over God in his life. He would give away what he loved the most if God asked, as he proved with the story of Isaac and the sacrifice. Abraham also proved it with the way that he handled parting with his nephew, Lot.

AVOIDING STRIFE AND TRUSTING GOD

Abraham was honorable. His motivation was to do things the right way and avoid strife. Instead of trying to gain the upper hand, he decided to trust God. He didn't survey the land to see how he could get the best deal out of the separation. He showed preference to his nephew and gave him first pick of the land. Why? For the sake of *peace*.

Abraham said, "Look, we are brethren and I don't want any strife between you and me, so please, separate yourself from me. Look at the whole of the land and take the side you want. If you go right, I'll go to the left. Look at all this land and choose what you want" (my paraphrase of Genesis 13:8).

How could Abraham give Lot first pick? Didn't he worry that his nephew was going to take the best land and leave him with the worst? No. Abraham didn't worry about the land! He worried about strife and handling things right. He trusted that God would bless him, no matter where he put his livestock, and no matter what land Lot picked.

Abraham didn't act like he was in competition with Lot either; he wasn't concerned that his nephew would do better financially. Why? Because Abraham wasn't looking at the sheep for provision. He had faith and was looking at *God* as Provider. At this growth point, he put his faith more in God than in land. Offering Lot first pick also showed Abraham as a graceful man who could not only handle prosperity, but also handle people.

THE GRASS IS ALWAYS GREENER OVER THE SEPTIC TANK

Lot wasn't so graceful. The Bible says in Genesis 13:10 that he *"lifted his eyes and beheld all the plain of Jordan, that it was well watered everywhere… as the garden of the LORD."* He made his choice based only on what his eyes saw. He took what looked like the best land from his uncle.

You remember where the Scripture says Lot pitched his tent, right? He was pointed right towards Sodom. Obviously, not only did the land beside Sodom look good to the eye, but the town itself must have also looked pretty good to the eye. So, here is another point I want you to see that we can learn from this story. Eyes can be deceiving.

Prosperity doesn't always come from the best looking thing out there. Don't just look with your eyes. Pray. Do the right thing in handling others so that you are known more for graciousness than ruthlessness. Let God lead you, knowing that wherever you go, you will prosper because God is with you. Even when the "land" or situation doesn't look as good as somebody else's, don't let that sway you. God can help you produce more with less!

Remember that a lot of not-so-pretty looking land has oil running underground. That's a parallel but the point is that you can't go solely by what you see. You're just going to have to do what you know to do and trust the God who trusts in you. Have faith in God! Have faith in yourself as His child. Do the right thing to keep your conscience clean.

> **Just because you can't see how the blessing will come doesn't mean it's impossible. And just because something looks like the best thing you ever saw doesn't mean it IS the best thing you'll ever get. Lot saw technicolor green grass right at the edge of Sodom!**

"The grass is always greener over the septic tank!"—that's what I've heard people say and it's funny, but also very true. Watch out for that sewer grass! If you read further, you'll notice that it wasn't long before Lot went from just pitching his tent *towards* Sodom to actually *living* there. That's right! He ended up living in a place synonymous with men who were "exceedingly wicked and sinful against the Lord." That was his choice, and he made it the moment he pointed himself in a wrong direction. He continued to make that choice with every step he took toward that wrong direction.

OBEDIENCE OPENS DOORS

Meanwhile, Abraham did the right thing and the moment he separated from Lot—which was exactly what God had asked him to do in telling him to get away from his kin in the very beginning—God started moving in his life even *MORE*. The Scripture doesn't talk about God speaking to Lot. Lot wasn't listening anyway! The Scripture shows us that it's the people who have ears to hear who actually *hear*. In other words, it's about listening.

God started talking to Abraham about what was going to bring him into even *more* blessing—full prosperity. Spiritually, physically, and financially, God's plan for Abraham (and for you as his seed) encompasses it ALL.

Genesis 13:14-17 tells of God speaking to Abraham about the Promised Land and descendants that would number the sands of the earth, if they could be counted. Again, this is full spiritual, physical, and financial prosperity that God is talking about. And when did Abraham hear about it? Only after he dealt with the discomfort of change. Only after he went back to what God had originally told him to do.

Obedience is powerful. It shows faith and humility. So, when you hit a growth point, what are you going to do?

> **I pray that you'll recognize growth points
> for what they are—necessary for your growth.
> While the discomfort of change is hard,
> obedience to God is the gateway
> to future blessings.**

Pray and trust God to guide you. Make a decision that no matter what things look like, you're going to do the right thing and that no matter what people-issues you may have to go through, you're going to act with grace. Strife does not have to be a part of your life. *You* choose to handle things right. *You* decide to trust God. *You* decide to look through the lens of faith in Him, instead of just looking at the situation in the natural.

Just like He did with Abraham, God will honor your choice to believe His Word. Obedience will open the door for more words from Him and more blessings on your life as you keep your eyes on Him and stay brave enough to walk by faith and not by sight.

Decide now that you're never going to let prosperity or success turn you toward a godless place in life, that your success will make you even more in awe of God's wonderful hand on your life. Never forget, if you succeed God's way, it's His Holy Spirit that is guiding you, challenging you, and taking care of the future as you move on to great adventures in faith!

Can you do this on your own? No! You can't do it on your own, but with God you can do anything. Jesus said ALL things are possible to them that believe. All means all! So, decide, "I'm choosing peace. I'm choosing to trust. I'm working hard but doing it God's way—the wise way!

CHAPTER 6

Establish in Yourself that God Can't Lie

"God is not a man, that He should lie; neither the son of man, that He should repent: hath He said, and shall He not do it? or hath He spoken, and shall He not make it good?"

Numbers 23:19

One of the greatest insights about God is found in that one small verse in Numbers 23:19. It lets us know in very plain terms that God is literally incapable of lying. There was no need for Jesus to repent of anything because there was no sin in Him. Settle this inside yourself: If God said something in His Word, He is not lying.

**Do your part and God will do His part.
Believe and act on His Word and God will
"Make It Good."**

If God's Word says you can be the lender and not the borrower, you can. Now, that seems unbelievable in this day and age of debt. If His Word says that you can be healed, you can. Now, that seems impossible in any age. If His Word says that you can love your enemies and even bless those that curse you, you can! Now, I know that is hard to imagine but with God, it's doable.

To go to the top God's way, you have to learn how to deal with doubt. Doubt! It's common but conquerable. Faith! It's uncommon but doable! When you are doing things God's way, doubts will still come up. It's natural. The Word says the natural mind doesn't understand the things of God and, in fact, it's foolishness to the mere brain. But we are much more than tissue and bone! We are a spirit, with a soul, housed in a body. If we just use one part of ourselves, we can't grasp truth. We must use and appreciate our whole being. We must grow.

Grass grows when rain stimulates it. Babies grow when they are fed. We grow in truth and wisdom for life and success when the Word of God stimulates us. That's why in order to conquer doubt, we must feed and water ourselves with the Word of God.

Faith in God Comes by Hearing His Word

You need faith in God to succeed God's way, and faith comes only one way.

"So then faith cometh by hearing, and hearing by the word of God."

Romans 10:17

If you don't repetitively hear the Word, you won't grow in faith. You need to hear what God has said in order to stir up the gift of God within you. The Word will fill your mind with wise principles and stoke the fires of your heart so that the power of the Holy Spirit within you can actually help you to be a doer of the Word. Faith without works is dead; it's pure vanity to think otherwise (James 2:20).

Doubts will come. It doesn't mean there is something wrong with your faith. This is the natural mind trying to process and grasp the things of the spirit. So, to succeed God's way and live at the top, you've got to deal with doubts, and let each one go just as easily as it comes.

The mind will try and spin the things of God to justify lack, sickness, misery, and whatever else may hold you back. Break the pattern by making a choice to let go of doubt and the fear that rises up when your mind tries to usurp your spirit.

How do you do this? You "cast down" every "imagination" and thing that comes into your mind that is against God. One way you do this is by simply not allowing yourself to spin in circles. Remember that the Word calls the devil the "author of confusion" and his area of expertise is spin! So, stop yourself. Don't fall for it! It's not in your best interest to side with the devil.

Choose to not contemplate what is contrary to God and His Word. Choose to say no to doubt and stop letting doubt in God take you for a ride. God is bigger that you can imagine. His thoughts are higher than your thoughts and His ways are higher than your ways (Isaiah 55:9). Don't set yourself up for failure by making an opinion about God that isn't true just because you don't yet grasp something in His Word. Pray for the eyes of your understanding to be opened (Ephesians 1:18). Trust God that He knows what He is talking about!

AIM FOR CHILDLIKE FAITH
SPEAK THE WORD, INSERT YOURSELF

After all, how can you gain anything *from* God if you don't *believe* God? You can't! So, you have to make a decision that God's Word is the final authority, in everything and especially in your particular situation. Make a choice to "only believe," as Jesus said (Mark 5:36, Luke 8:50). It's childlike faith that you should aim for each day, no matter in what area of life you are trying to go to the top. Not childish doubt!

**None of us are God's adults; we are His children.
Stay open and in awe of His power and ability
knowing that He can work through you.**

Believe what the Word says, because God can't lie. He can give you wells that you didn't dig and vineyards that you didn't plant, houses filled with things you didn't provide (Deuteronomy 6:11). He is the Provider! He is the One who gives you the ability to produce wealth and establish His covenant on the earth (Deuteronomy 8:18).

God is the One who causes you to be blessed in the city and blessed in the field, blessed coming in and blessed going out. It's God who blesses your children and who blesses your possessions. Even if enemies come at you one way, He's the One who causes them to flee seven ways! This is your God, the One who commands the blessing to come on you in your storehouse and in everything you set your hand to do (Deuteronomy 28:2-8).

God alone is the One who has made you the head and not the tail, above and not beneath (Deuteronomy 28:13). Don't doubt these things. Believe these things! God is on your side, and so you should endeavor to be on your side, too! Remember, a double-minded man is unstable in ALL his ways (James 1:8) and that's what doubt does to you—it fosters instability. Refuse that junk!

Doubt Your Doubts!

What's the best thing you can do when doubts come into your mind? Doubt them! I've been saying that for over thirty years because it's true; you have to doubt your doubts! Doubt what's doubting *God*! Doubt what's doubting *you*! That may not be good English and yes, it's a tongue-twister, but it's true.

Whatever the problem, look to the Word. Study to show yourself approved so that you need not be ashamed, and you can rightly divide the Word of truth (2 Timothy 2:15). Get all the scriptures you can on whatever area you want to climb and rise to the top. Then, when thoughts arise that are contrary to God's best, say "I doubt that!" and then quote the Word of God that applies to your situation.

If you're feeling weak, don't let your mind rotate "I can't do this" over and over. No, say, "I doubt that! I can do ALL things through Christ who strengthens me! God is showing Himself strong through me now, today, right now. Holy Spirit, I may feel weak but I will say that I AM strong!" (Philippians 4:13; Joel 3:10).

Use your mouth. Speak well *of* yourself *to* yourself every day by using the Word of God.

After all, if you're not on your own side, how do you think you're going to be able to get to where you want to be in life? You have to align yourself with what God says. *"I know the thoughts that I think toward you,"* God says. He has plans to give you a future and a hope (Jeremiah 29:11). God is thinking good thoughts about you—agree with Him!

Don't Tear Yourself Down

If you want to succeed God's way, stop tearing yourself down in your own mind and with your own mouth. It's pointless and confusing and you won't get to the top doing it. It's not enough to just be prosperous; you need to be fully prosperous and that means being in harmony with yourself, too. You can enjoy peace of mind and joy as you go along your way in life.

This fullness that God has for you as you journey to the top is worth working for, but if you waste your life tearing yourself down in your own mind instead of lifting yourself up with the Word, you will miss out on God's best. You'll miss opportunities. You'll miss noticing the goodness in life. You'll miss others along the way who could really use your help and influence in their lives, too. Your mindset doesn't just affect you, it also affects whomever you come into contact with, so you can either cast a shadow or bring light wherever you go.

The Word should be a light in your heart and a light on your path. Let it do its work by putting it first place. Make it so that you don't even have room in your mind to tear yourself down. You are going somewhere in this life!

> **Don't throw stones in your own path by beating yourself up—there is love and mercy in God! No matter where you came from or where you are now, you are going UP! Let God lead you to peace with His Word.**

Work for peace in yourself. Let the Word shine its light inside you. It'll bring up things you haven't thought about. It'll show you where you need hope and healing. Then, it will douse you in a love like you've never known before. It will lift your heaviness. Push through in prayer and joy will burst out of your spirit, lifting you up, right where you belong.

Peace is in the Lord, and you work for your own peace by putting your faith in the Lord. That's why you put yourself in those scriptures you find—because it IS personal. It's between God and you and the overflow will affect your family, your friends, and everyone you come into contact with. The truth can change your life, one day at a time. But first you have to read it, say it, and let it clear out the junk as God's truth rises to the top.

Doubts about God and yourself are just weights you don't need. They are just trying to steal, kill, and destroy God's best for your life. So don't let any of that doubt junk ping-pong around in your head—that is the opposite of trusting God. Bring every thought that tries to rise up against the knowledge of God in your life into captivity and speak the Word in faith. That's trusting God. Establish in yourself that God can't lie. Period. End of story. This will bring peace and free your mind up to focus on what you want—His best spiritually, physically, and financially!

What Are You Saying About God?

Tests will come. You will feel the pressure to give up and quit on the road to the top. You will hear what you *really* believe when that time comes, so be a spectator for a bit when you get down and lose it for minute. Check out what comes out of your mouth when things don't go the way you want them to go. What do you say about God then?

The words coming out of your mouth in times of pressure will reveal what's hidden in your heart. Remember Matthew 12:34?

"For out of the abundance of the heart the mouth speaketh."

Always choose to praise God instead of speaking evil of God. This is very important. I've heard so many Christians speak bad things about God. Sometimes they do it because they don't know better—they have been taught that He's not really good and they perpetuate a wrong doctrine. Other times they do it out of anger, disappointment, or frustration. They blame God for something that went wrong in life. I can honestly say that I haven't done that. Sure, sometimes I have wondered if God was listening to me (and He was), but I didn't resort to speaking bad things about Him. I always assumed I just didn't know or understand something. You see, some people think I'm arrogant but I'm not; I'm just confident in God's ability to do what He said, and I'm confident in my ability as His child to walk in His Word.

WHERE MY CONFIDENCE COMES FROM

My confidence comes from the fact that I've sown the Word deep into my heart. I've put the Word of God first place for a long time and all that "hearing and hearing by the Word of God" has made a huge impact on me.

God has brought me into a place of soundness of mind and confidence in Him. Once I decided to take God at His Word years ago, I started to work on dealing with doubt and I found overcoming it pretty easy. I could doubt the Creator of the universe, try to prove Him wrong, and be miserable in my confusion or I could accept that God is right and His Word is truth. I chose to accept the latter! God is God!

God loves me. I refuse to let doubt come into me about it. Why? Again, the Word is first place in my life and I've established in myself that God cannot lie. If He said it, it's a done deal.

> **If God said I'm made in His image, then I am.**
> **If He says I'm the head and not the tail, then I am.**
> **If He says that He knit me in my mother's womb**
> **and my body is wonderfully made, then it is!**
> **Believe this Word for yourself and see how**
> **it changes your life.**

If God says that you've been redeemed from the hand of the enemy, then you are. If He says don't fear because you've been redeemed and He's called you by name, then don't fear. You've been redeemed and He's called you by name saying, "You are Mine!" This is your Father talking to you. Listen to Him!

If God is for you, who can be against you? Where can you go to get away from His love? What can separate you from it? You're chosen! You're a new creature in Christ! Old things are passed away and all things have become new! You are dead to sin and alive in Christ! You're more than a conqueror and, through Jesus, guess what? You win!

Do you see what I'm doing here? I'm inserting you in the scripture, and the more you do this for yourself personally—at home, in your car, when you are getting ready to go to work, looking in the bathroom mirror even—the more you will get fired up about your potential in this life. Part of knowing who you are as a person is knowing Who you belong to, and that would be the Lord.

Scripture is alive with power. Use it to stir yourself up and it will help you in so many ways. Give yourself that firm foundation in life. Your future is worth it!

CHAPTER 7

~

The Internal Force that Activates External Circumstances

Faith in God is an internal human force that activates external circumstances. You could almost imagine it to be like sound waves coming out of your spirit/heart and mind/mouth, pushing through the atmosphere around you and going to work for you.

> *"For verily I say unto you, That whosoever shall <u>say</u> unto this mountain, Be thou removed, and be thou cast into the sea; and shall <u>not doubt in his heart</u>, but shall <u>believe</u> that those things which he saith shall <u>come to pass</u>; he shall <u>have whatsoever</u> he saith."*
>
> Mark 11:23, emphasis mine

This teaching from Jesus tells us how to get rid of what we don't want—mountains that stand in the way of having what we do want. In life, many times, we must remove what distracts our view. The mountain is distracting.

Distractions come to steal your future moment by moment. Christ's teaching about how to remove these mountains in our life never once mentions begging and pleading with God for help. Jesus never taught us that begging was the way to receive from God. No, He had a very specific method that He wanted us to learn to do, in order that we might grow and live like God's children.

"Say unto this mountain" involves your mouth—it's a confident act of your will. "Be thou removed" is telling the mountain in your life that you want it gone. "And be cast into the sea" is telling it where it should go—out of your sight.

This method of removal is not something you do silently. Jesus was specific that you needed to use words and speak something into the air around that mountain. God made you powerful. Even when you feel weak, you are actually strong. The Word says when we feel weak, we must (like Jesus taught with the mountain) speak and say that we are strong.

Words alone won't work though, because Jesus says in His teaching that to get results we must not doubt in our heart, but actually believe what we are saying. How many people go through life saying one thing but believing another? That's discord within your own being and nothing works well when strife is present.

Harmony is necessary within your being in order to "move mountains." This harmony is what perfects the force of faith so that it can do what it was designed by God to do: Move things out. Move things in. Change your life for the better. According to Christ, this doesn't happen when your head is fighting with your heart; you must be aligned with God's Word and with yourself.

LEARN TO ENJOY SPEAKING TO MOUNTAINOUS SITUATIONS

God gave you an incredible mind, your ability to imagine and dream is a wonderful gift from God. Do you ever wonder about its purpose? What would you do if you had no ability to imagine? There is power in imagining.

Jesus used parables to give us pictures for a reason. A mountain is big. It stands between you and what's on the other side. Anything that is not God's best for your life could be compared to a mountain, and I like to visualize things like that moving out of my way in my mind. I like to imagine. I allow myself the luxury of dreaming of my faith in God bringing to pass exactly whatever I need and desire into my life.

I know that my words are a key element to making things come to pass in my life because Jesus said so, and so I must move the internal doubt out of the way so that I can use my faith in God on the external mountains standing in the way of God's best. I want my faith to work. I want results. We all do, and so we have to do the work inside.

When you get to the place of *"shall not doubt in his heart,"* you are on your way to having *"whatsoever he saith."*

There are two kinds of doubt—"head doubt" and "heart doubt." It's not doubt in your head that is the real problem, that is just random thoughts coming up against the truth of God's Word and they are easy to fix. You deal with them one at a time as they come up.

This is what 2 Corinthians 10:5 tells us about handling thoughts of doubt that come into your head: *"Casting down imaginations, and every high thing that exalteth itself against the knowledge of God, and bringing into captivity every thought to the obedience of Christ."* There is an effort to it but it can literally change your entire life if you simply practice this amazing truth from the Word. I'll share more in a moment about that, but let's get to the kind of doubt Jesus was talking about in Mark 11:23.

"Heart doubt" is a root. It comes when you allow "head doubt" to spin for too long, and you enforce it with your own words to such a degree that it sinks down and becomes a fully formed falsity in your heart. You may think it's true but it's not. It's a lie that you repeated until you believed it.

**Anything that exalts itself up above the
knowledge of God is a lie. Doubts are the mind's
way of attempting to protect you and help you
survive in a fallen world—but anything that is
opposed to God is not helping you...
it's hindering you.**

You will have to conquer doubt if you want to live at the top
and you do that by letting the Word of God pull up the roots, so
to speak. If you find you have true "heart doubt" like that, find
a scripture that says the truth you are internally fighting against
and start planting that verse in your heart right alongside the
doubt!

You see, you won't get anywhere if you live in denial. Denial
is saying that the root doesn't exist. Even a fool can see it exists
if he looks into your heart! So, don't deny where you are right
now. Deny the doubt!

How do you close that gap between what God says and what
you really believe? By hearing and hearing by the Word of God.
So think of your heart like a garden and sow that scripture into
yourself. Do it daily, repetitively. Every single time you rehearse
the truth, you negate a little more of the lie. Truth cancels out
doubt. But you have to meditate on the Word to continue to
enforce new beliefs in God's truth.

CONQUERING DOUBT ISN'T JUST SOME INTERNAL FIGHT IT'S ABOUT LETTING GO OF FEAR AND LEARNING TRUTH

The more you do this, the more you will recognize "heart doubt" whenever you think, *I don't know if I believe this.* Immediately, that's when you should simply let the thought go and again, reiterate the truth of God's Word to yourself.

You aren't fighting yourself and trying to convince yourself. You are learning what truth is and re-establishing faith in God in your own heart. If the disappointments of life itself and the constant onslaught of doubt in the world have done anything, they've likely chipped away at the childlike nature of your heart. So, shift yourself to where you need to be in order to live at the top and succeed God's way.

> **If you struggle with doubt, consider every Scripture like medicine for your soul— words that are re-training you to think the right way (God's way), instead of the wrong way, (this fallen world's way).**

The Word will do its job if you discipline yourself to do yours, because the Word is compared to a sword in the scripture and it's sharp enough to cut that doubt right out of you! There is anointing and power in the Word when it is spoken in faith. Speak it in faith over your own heart. Rip out doubt from the root!

Pulling Fresh Weeds and Trading Thoughts

Fleeting thoughts of doubt are those head doubts I mentioned, and they are easy to get rid of because they have no root. Think of them like a fresh weed in the yard; easy to pull out and keep on walking!

You start by noticing that the thought opposed to what God said just shot up in your mind. Noticing is half the battle! Most people let the weeds run wild; they just spin in doubt, and spend years thinking about stuff that won't bring them any closer to what they really want in life. So, this is how you reel in a thought and pick out fleeting doubts. You just trade them out for a better thought—really, it's that easy.

> **As doubts pop up, you can simply trade them in.
> You just shift your focus to what God said instead
> of dwelling on every little lie that pops up
> in your head against the Word.**

What kind of thought should you replace the doubtful thought with? Anything you want that doesn't negate God's truth. What are you believing for? What do you want? Find yourself a scripture that corresponds and use it—speak it with your mouth, too. The Scripture says:

> *"Finally, brethren, <u>whatsoever</u> things are <u>true</u>, whatsoever things are <u>honest</u>, whatsoever things are <u>just</u>, whatsoever things are <u>pure</u>, whatsoever things are <u>lovely</u>, whatsoever*

things are of good report; if there be any virtue, and if there be any praise, think on these things. Those things, which ye have both learned, and received, and heard, and seen in me, do: and the God of peace shall be with you."

Philippians 4:8-9, emphasis mine

Now, what does "whatsoever" mean? It means whatsoever! All day long, get into the habit of trading your thoughts—when you get a bad one trade it in for a good one. That good thought, if it's the Word of God, will change your life. But, *any* good thought about any good thing in the world is a better thought than doubt, misery, sadness, anxiety, whatever is plaguing your mind and clogging up the wheels of your godly success!

You have a choice. Choose the good thought over the bad thought. Choose a scripture over a fresh head-doubt. Choose life and not death. Do these things daily, in little increments.

If you do this routinely, as you are just going about your day, you'll build a habit of thinking on things that are good for you instead of bad for you. The more you do it, the more effortless it will become. You will be drawn to what's good for you, and that's with God in every area of your life. By letting go of thoughts that don't lead to anything good, you are also freeing up some space in your head to deliberately think new thoughts, as well as allow for new imaginations and dreams that are not fear-based.

God loves you—this is the primary foundational truth. Everything good is in your best interest because everything good came from Him, and He loves you and wants the best for you. When you catch yourself not believing Him, you are just shooting yourself in the foot and making it harder to walk along in life. God wants your steps to be energetic. The joy of the Lord is called your strength for a reason. There is nothing joyful about turmoil in the mind, so work on this! Think and speak the goodness of God's Word. Let the bad flow out and the good flow in! Trade in your thoughts!

THE POWER OF THE MIND

I heard a doctor say something on television not long ago about pathological liars that was astounding. He said that some people lie so much that they actually convince themselves of their own lie—they honestly believe that the lie they created is the truth. In other words, they said the lie so many times (not only to others but to themselves) that the lie seeded down into their heart and for them, the lie ceased to be a lie and became truth to them. That's the power of the mind that God created, but working in the *wrong* direction—this is self-deception!

Jesus revealed the right, pure, and godly way to use this mental ability when He encouraged believers to not only *believe* what is unbelievable and impossible, but also to *speak* it with their mouths and *not doubt* their hearts. That's what moving mountains is all about, and God wouldn't tell you that you could do it if you couldn't do it!

Your faith is an energy force. You were created in God's image, and in Genesis the story of creation shows us that God used words to form worlds. This is a lesson to us about how to change our world.

There is no confusion in God. Jesus isn't arguing with the Father and the Holy Spirit isn't arguing with Jesus! That's a joke, but you understand what I'm saying, I hope. Internal conflict stops the force of faith.

Focusing the force of faith towards what is TRUE—not what is deceiving or a lie—is our birthright as human beings. When we become children of God by opening ourselves to Him and accepting Christ's sacrifice, we are born again and we now are able to see that the portion of faith inside of us is enough. It's enough to do big things inside our heart and outside in the world.

We draw close to God. We read His Word and get to know His truth. These things resonate within us and the Holy Spirit brings things up in our own heart. I can't say this enough, we must choose to focus on His truth, seeding it into our hearts by continually hearing the Word of God. Repetitively, we remind ourselves and repetitively we speak it out with the sole purpose of aligning ourselves with God and all the good things He established so that our lives go in the right direction.

Remember how Lot pitched his tent where he really didn't need to be? His focus was not on the best thing for his life, and his life went in that direction. To get the best results for yourself and your life, you must focus on the best things for yourself and your life. You must speak the best things *over* yourself and *to* yourself.

The best thing you can say over yourself is what God has already said about you, because there is no higher love than God's. He loves you because He is love. The only reason you can love is because He loved you first. Jesus gave His life for you and His blood was shed for not only the remission of your sin, but to open the door for you to experience God on the highest level. That level is the one of Father and child, and your Father really does know exactly who you are down to the hairs on your head. His Spirit flows through you and will help you.

God is pure, righteous, and loving and He cannot lie. It's impossible for Him to lie. God does not coerce or manipulate. He loves. He guides. He cares. And He has established truths for human beings that are constant. They do not change. So you can set your mind at ease and go about your day, trading thoughts and taking good opportunities as He brings them your way—and He will!

SOW GOD'S SPIRIT AND REAP THE BENEFITS

What you sow, you will reap. If you are sowing the Word and good thoughts and seeking full harmony with yourself and God, your life is going to show it.

You have fruit that is being produced in your life all the time, so it's wise to take a look at yourself and see just what you are putting out there into the world. Can people come up and eat from your life and leave feeling better than when they came? Or do they leave you like they just bit a lemon?

What you put into your mind and heart will come out of your mouth and it will filter into your daily ways. The Word tells us that there are attributes that can be compared to the fruit of God's Spirit flowing in your life, because that's what you want.

> **This isn't about being a good person. It's about being a God-led person! Both do good deeds, but one has the Holy Spirit leading and anointing him for those good works.**

That's what we should aim for as believers—the energy of God emanating out of our spirit into this world, shifting things like waves, penetrating the air and atmosphere with fearless faith in God and good works!

Galatians 5:22-23 tells you what the fruit of God's Spirit is like so that you can check to see if these things are flowing in you: *"But the fruit of the Spirit is love, joy, peace, longsuffering, gentleness, goodness, faith, meekness, temperance: against such there is no law."*

The more you focus on God and His truthful Word, the more you will see these fruit coming up and out of your heart into your everyday life. The more you sow them, the more you reap the benefits—they have ripple effects in your life and in the lives of those you encounter. You have no clue how much influence on this world you have, just as the smallest rock makes a ripple. The tiniest faith moves mountains. The smallest shift changes perspective.

REPENT AND RELEASE

So, how do you know if you mess up in the little things? Your spirit will immediately let you know. You'll feel the tug of conviction. You'll notice in your spirit that you veered off course. And what do you do if you mess up in the big things? You do the same thing for both: Repent and release. Ask the Lord for forgiveness and move on, going right back to where you were before you missed the mark. The blood of Jesus can and will immediately wash any transgression away the moment that you repent. But, you have to release yourself in order to start again.

Don't let anybody, even your own mind, put a guilt trip on you for what the blood of Jesus has already washed away. If guilt tries to rise up, acknowledge it is there and then trade in that thought and reinforce it with the truth—God loves you, and you have been forgiven. Old things are passed away and all things have become new. The blood is enough. It is enough for all of us.

Repent and release, and then do exactly what you should do to point yourself in the right direction. Keep trading in thoughts, speaking to the mountains and moving forward daily with the internal energy of faith. Then, your eyes will open wider and wider in childlike faith and you will see results that you could not imagine, even with that great mind the Lord gave you!

The more you move yourself in the right direction for your life by accepting that God loves you— and His love is Who He is and at the core of His anointing—the more you will find it easy to believe and receive the BEST God has for you.

Never forget that our faith is not based on self-made or man-made lies! Our faith is not deception or a vehicle for self-deception. Our faith is based on the God of ALL and His Son, Jesus Christ, and the sacrifice Christ made for the whole world, so that we could come into right standing and begin to live as we were always meant to live—inside of God's blessing and fearless in our faith!

GOD IS ON YOUR SIDE
YOU NEED TO BE ON YOUR SIDE, TOO

One day, every knee will bow and every tongue confess that Jesus is Lord. Jesus Christ and Him crucified is the only way, truth, and life for us in this world.

*"I am the way, the truth and the life:
no man cometh unto the Father, but by me."*

John 14:6

Jesus is our Teacher—He is the way, the truth, and the life. Trust Him. Believe His method—*say* to the mountain and *do not doubt* in your heart, because whatever you *say*, if you *believe*, it *will* come to pass. You are going to have what you say, so say good things with the force of your faith.

Nobody can pry this teaching away from me. I don't serve a stingy God and neither do you! He's not just living at the top— He *is* the TOP! God is on our side and we have to be on our own side, too! Use the Mark 11:23 instruction and live well—don't be afraid of having "whatsoever things" you want, because there is absolutely nothing wrong with "things!"

CHAPTER 8

～

There Is Nothing Wrong with "Things"

Remember Abraham. What was he? VERY RICH! Like I said in chapter four, the Scripture even tells us *what* he was rich in and it was tangible, material earthly blessings. Abraham wasn't only spiritually rich. He was financially rich.

Today in the church, people are so afraid of believing God for material things, as if it is against God in some way. This is why I feel I must reiterate this point before we go further. If God didn't approve of material blessings, the Scripture wouldn't record Him blessing Abraham with an abundance of gold, silver, and livestock. God doesn't give things He hates or is against.

So, let's make this personal. If God is against *you* having "things," He wouldn't have blessed *anybody* with "things" because God is no respecter of persons (Acts 10:34). What He does for others, He will do for you, too. God is not a man that can lie. God also favors no man or woman over another. He loves us all equally. But is our faith in Him and His Word equal? No.

We are all at different stages. We are all affected by whatever we allow ourselves to be affected by. We can choose to sow the Word, speak the Word, and believe—or not. We can choose to walk in the Spirit, live by the Spirit, and do things according to the Spirit—or not. The blood of Jesus washes us all clean in the same way, but what we do with the faith we've been given is up to us.

So, how much will you let God do? He's not going to honor doubt and wavering faith. That will just toss us around and won't get the results we need to prosper God's way. What we do and say is up to us. It's not up to God. We are the ones who have to fill our heart with His truth and our mouth with confidence in His ability to make us rich—spiritually, physically, financially, and in every other way that we want Him to make us rich.

In other words, we choose where we pitch our tent! Do we want to go towards God's goodness and life, and the abundance that follows? Or do we want to pitch our tent towards strife, ungodliness, and death.

God isn't a respecter of persons, but He is a respecter of *faith*.

Jesus Was Revolutionary, Not Religious
Follow Christ and Avoid Control

Jesus was not an enemy of desire. You were created in God's image and He *desires* a relationship with you. He wants love, connection, and to show you His goodness in this life and throughout eternity. So, God has desires. You have them, too, and there isn't a thing wrong with that.

> **When your desires line up with God's, the richness of that kind of life is noticeable in ALL areas of life. It's not just spiritual. It's physical. It's financial. It's EVERYTHING. Seeking first the kingdom is when ALL of these things can be added to you.**

Let that dumb, old, religious spirit of holy poverty just roll off of your mind like water off a duck's back. It's irrelevant. It's not true. God wants the best for you and His best isn't a broke wallet or a hungry belly!

How do you get what you want then? Not the world's way, but God's way? You look to Jesus, the Author and Finisher of your faith. If you listen, if you seek to know the truth, if you honor Him and simply believe and do it, you'll see results. There's no other way around it.

If you hash it out in your mind looking for loopholes to give credence to doubt, you're not going to get anything His way. If you argue with Jesus, you won't get anything. You can't be in strife with the Son of the Living God and succeed! Are you living in a dream world? Let the elevator go to the top!

Jesus taught how to receive what we desire, and it's revolutionary, but it ain't religious! Jesus continually smacked against religious hypocrisy that is born out of a human man's need to control others—that's fear. Fear is the opposite of faith. So when you see somebody going full force against the teachings of Jesus in a religious mindset, you have to remember that Jesus dealt with this constantly in His earthly ministry. He's still dealing with that today, people who might mean well or might not, but still have the same problem. They're wrong. If you want to know the definition of "right" it's called Jesus—righteousness personified!

When you start believing Jesus' teachings, expect people to come against you and try to talk down His teaching. Ignore them. Don't even fight. Share the truth if you see they can hear it and if not, just move along. Remember that Jesus didn't waste time trying to convince people He was the Son of God. You never hear Him in Scripture saying, "Come on! Believe Me!" No. He taught. He prayed. He loved. He often was very to-the-point with people who wanted to trip Him up and He was also often silent. In other words, if people want to argue, don't let them find a willing debating partner in you. You have been called to peace, and not to strife!

Whatever some people fear, they try to control and what they can't control, they will criticize, so refuse to let them control you. God has good things in store for you!

The truth comes with persecution sometimes, but it's worth it. You know, when I teach what Jesus taught, some religious people want to hurt me over it. It's uncomfortable to them, and sometimes, they get downright nasty! I've had them physically try to hurt me over it. I don't care. I'm free—the truth has set me free, and that means I'm free indeed (John 8:36).

No chains of bondage will hold me down when Christ has already spoken the truth that I can have whatsoever things I desire when I pray. God is for me, and not against me. So, who cares what people think?

As believers, we should care what the Lord thinks the most! Nothing Jesus taught us is outside of our best interest because He was here doing the will of the Father, and your Father God knows the thoughts He has for you. They are only to give you a future and a hope—that's good!

> "Therefore I say unto you, What things soever ye desire, when ye pray, believe that ye receive them, and ye shall have them."
>
> Mark 11:24

Now, I want you to study that verse until you know it by heart and until you grasp the simple but astounding truth of it. Notice that you bring your desires to God in your times of prayer. Let's talk about that first. Prayer is not seeing where the words may splatter. It's a focused and active state of approaching God with purpose.

How to Approach God
Praying and Aligning Yourself with the Source

Look at the words *"when ye pray"*—notice that Jesus assumes you will pray! A lot of people don't pray. Start if you haven't been doing it much. Prayer must be a part of the life of a believer who wants his desires met. God can get something to you, but not if you don't connect with Him. He's the Source and this is a relationship you are cultivating, not just to get desires met, but also to become closer to Him.

God already knows you through and through. Prayer makes it easier for you to get to know Him. Don't get caught up in "sounding good when you pray" because that's not the point. Be honest with yourself and pray from your heart.

There are two things you should do when you pray; start with them, and you will be more effective. Psalm 100:4 says, *"Enter into his gates with thanksgiving, and into his courts with praise: be thankful unto him, and bless his name."* Don't just start telling God what you desire. The Word says to enter His gates with thanksgiving first, which means you start in a state of thankfulness to Him. Then, you enter into His courts with praise.

Thankfulness will bust through a mind that just wants to complain and focus on the problem. Thanksgiving starts you off on the right foot. You can be thankful for a lot of things in life, but also try to express just being thankful for Who God *is* to you. This gets your mind out of the position of lack where you are focused on what you don't have Get out of the mental position of lack! Even when you pray, pitch your tent towards what is good. God is good!

**A thankful heart is extremely powerful!
It's pointing your mind in the direction of power—
God is the Source of all power and nothing
is impossible with Him.**

Next, "enter His courts with praise." You might notice how easy it will be to flow into praising God after being thankful. Praising God is it's own subject entirely, taking your focus upwards to God as your Father, His Son as your mediator, and His Holy Spirit as your ever-present help.

The Holy Spirit moves when you praise God. Make sure that you are praising God from your heart—the source of who you are connecting and praising the Source of everything. That's praise. You might need to stay in that state of praise for a little longer. It's up to you. Thanksgiving and praise are two of the most empowering things you can do for yourself because there is something about them that puts your heart in the right position to receive from God.

God will reveal Himself if you are open to Him as *El Shaddai*—the all-sufficient, all-bountiful, Almighty God; the One who is more than enough and can take care of you. Looking at Him, you start to lose sight of the former thought that maybe He's not enough. God is more than enough. In fact, He's too much!

Remember, no matter what you need or desire from the Lord, it's not your job to tell Him "how" to do it. It's your job to believe Him and be obedient to His Word. Any thoughts that start going in the direction of "how God should do this for me" are fruitless thoughts that don't matter and only muddy up your prayer life. Let God be God. Don't tell Him how to do His job!

Now, you can do the next step to get yourself in alignment with the Source and ready to receive. This one isn't easy, but it's of the utmost importance.

CHECK YOUR HEART
PUT A SPOTLIGHT ON YOURSELF

Sometimes, we bury things in our heart that we don't want to deal with. We ignore the faces and situations of people in our lives who have made our way more difficult, and who we resent for it. But to ignore that feeling of resentment and anger that's hidden in our heart is a mistake if we want to prosper God's way. These things need to be made "right" and prayer is the way to really check in to see what's going on.

In the past, when I've questioned why something wasn't working, I've found that stopping and assessing myself this way—allowing the Holy Spirit to put a spotlight on my own life—showed that I had overlooked something that needed correcting. Sometimes it was just a small thing, but it bothered me enough that I needed to change. Other times it was something I'd nearly forgotten, but the Holy Spirit reminded me it was in my heart.

**Each time it was something I needed to make right
or someone I needed to release so that my prayers
would work more effectively.**

Once I realized that I couldn't succeed without doing this,
it became so easy because I want God's best and I'm not about
to let what someone else did or said about me affect my ability
to receive from God. No offence is worth my future! You should
develop the same mindset when it comes to unforgiveness.

> *"And when ye stand praying, forgive, if ye have ought
> against any: that your Father also which is in heaven may
> forgive you your trespasses."*

Mark 11:25

Unforgiveness is the biggest stumbling block for Christians. It literally stops your progress from the inside out. What
is unforgiveness? It's a mind focused on the past, and the past
never sees the future. It's a heart stuck in a loop, and you can't go
anywhere if all you are doing is going in circles inside yourself.
Break free! Even if what they said or did was horribly wrong,
let the Holy Spirit help you to release them of it all. Those past
frustrations and anger with people will steal your good future.
Your eyes must be looking forward if you are to achieve anything
new, not backward.

The Apostle Paul tells us in Philippians 3:13 to forget those
things that are behind and reach forward to the things that are

ahead. It's necessary to do this in order to reach for the prize of your high calling in Christ Jesus. This means your destiny is linked to your ability to let people go from the internal judgment you have against them for the wrongs they've done. You are not God. You are not their judge. Let Him deal with them—you deal with *you*!

I'm not saying forgiveness is easy, but I am saying that it is a must not only for success or receiving from God, but for your own heart and peace of mind. You have no idea how much weight you are carrying around until you let it go.

You can't remain in a state of grudge-holding and unforgiveness if you intend to receive God's best because you need for there to be zero hindrance between you and the Lord. Holding on to unforgiveness is like putting blockages in your own path. This is like being in strife with God Himself. The Father loves people and Jesus plainly stated that His Father will *not* forgive *you* of your mess-ups until you forgive others of their mess-ups. This is a very hard truth, but it's still the truth. Accept this as just a fact of life.

Your forgiveness is directly and forever tied to the forgiveness you give others.

So, it is a trade off—you need exactly what you must give. Remember that forgiving someone doesn't mean you are accepting that what he or she did was right. They may be purely wrong in every single way. You may not have done anything at all, or you may have. Either way, it doesn't mean you have to accept and agree with the one who wronged you.

Forgiveness is a spiritual concept of releasing someone, regardless of whether they deserve it or not. In fact, they might *not* deserve it! But, then again, neither do you—none of us deserve what Jesus did. His was an act of grace and the grace of God is amazing: He loved you when you were yet a sinner and He sent His Son to die for you.

So think of it like this: Forgiveness doesn't have much to do with the one who wronged you, but it has everything to do with your personal need to be right with the Lord. It's time to get rid of those internal blockages. You don't have to do it alone.

THE ONE ACCEPTABLE SPOTLIGHT

God has given you a helper: The Holy Spirit. Ask Him to reveal whatever is hiding out in your heart; do this after you have entered His gates with thanksgiving in your heart and into His courts with praise. By then, your heart will be open to hear. The Holy Spirit will never lead you on a wrong path—He will always guide you in truth. You can trust Him.

John 16:13-15 says, *"Howbeit when he, the Spirit of truth, is come, he will <u>guide you into all</u> <u>truth</u>: for he <u>shall not speak of</u> <u>himself</u>; but whatsoever he shall hear, that shall he speak: and he will <u>shew you things</u> to come. He <u>shall glorify me</u>: for he shall receive of mine, and shall shew it unto you. All things that the Father hath are mine: therefore said I, that he shall take of mine, and shall shew it unto you"* (emphasis mine).

Isn't that comforting? Just that verse alone ought to make everyone become a Christian! The Holy Spirit is your connection to God in prayer—He says what He hears God say, and guides you in all truth. So, when you pray, ask the Holy Spirit to reveal anything about yourself that is blocking your way in life. I promise that if you are honest with yourself and allow Him to speak to you, He will show you exactly what you need to do to make things right.

When you pray, you may want to speak it aloud with your mouth so that your mind hears what your mouth is saying. You may need to actually say the infraction that caused you to resent a person. The hurt may come pouring out. If so, know that the Holy Spirit will not leave you alone and will help guide you to a place of peace if you don't run away from Him.

**Don't run away from what's bothering you.
Face the fear of letting go. Your heart may ache
as you face it, but you will be set free!
There is peace on the other side of forgiveness.**

The Holy Spirit can literally pull those deep roots up and out of your heart—forgiveness *is* healing. Your physical body will even feel the effects of forgiveness. Unforgiveness is a state of spiritual and emotional stress. The longer you hold onto it, the more bound you are and sometimes you don't even realize it. You've walked with that limp for so long, you think it's normal. It's not. Let the Holy Spirit become your divine

Guide. Healing from heart pain is for you, and a better and more joyful life is for you.

When the Spirit prompts you to forgive, do it. And if He brings up other things you need to do, do them. Saying something you should have said, doing something you should have done, apologizing, giving, helping...whatever it is that the Holy Spirit brings up in your heart, do it. Clear the air in your life! Clear the air in your heart!

The act of obedience alone will open your heart. Doing what the Lord said (forgiving in your heart) and doing what the Holy Spirit tells you (making things right in your life) will break down the hindrances so that you can actually have the successful life you want.

So, now, what do you want?

CHAPTER 9

What Do You WANT? You Can Have "What Things Soever Ye Desire"

Desire—the word alone freaks out people in the church! Immediately sirens go off in their mind. They think negatively about the word "desire" as if it is something bad, full of only negative qualities, and at total odds against the will of a holy God. Nothing could be further from the truth.

Do you ever notice that the world is against godly prosperity? Do you notice the church often is, too? They have taken the bait—hook, line, and sinker—that godly people must not be interested in "things" at all. They believe that poverty is holy and a blessing…except at *their* house. That's kind of funny, but it's no joke!

Have you ever noticed that
the church is ok with you being poor,
but the church itself cannot be poor?

It's almost as if the church is saying, "You've got to give all your money to the church! Bless God! Now, you go home and starve!" Do you see how asinine this kind of thinking is? If the church thinks money's so bad, why are they receiving offerings today? Why do they receive donations?

The truth is that there is nothing evil about money. It's the LOVE of money that is the root of all evil (1 Timothy 6:10). And you can love money, even if you don't have any!

The love of money is not just a "rich man's" disease—it affects people of every economic bracket. If you love something more than you love God, you're off course. We are believers! God comes first, and when our priorities are in order, all the "things" we need and desire are then able to be added unto us (Matthew 6:33; Luke 12:31).

"WANT" AND "DESIRE" ARE NOT UNGODLY WORDS

Things aren't bad. Desire isn't bad. God has both, things and desires. Heaven has gold streets and gates of pearl, that's "things." God desires for us to know Him and the Scripture tells us, *"Eye hath not seen, nor ear heard, neither have entered into the heart of man, the things which God hath prepared for them that love Him"* (1 Corinthians 2:9). When we get to Heaven, we will see even more of God's desires in action. Since God has desires and you are created in His image, you also have desires; this means that "want" isn't a bad word!

> **If "desire" or "things" were innately wrong and ungodly, Jesus Christ wouldn't have given us instruction on how to fulfill our desires and have things.**

Do you believe the words of Jesus? Jesus took the limits off when He spoke this truth, *"Therefore I say unto you, What things soever ye desire when ye pray, believe that ye receive them, and ye shall have them"* (Mark 11:24).

I taught on prayer earlier because that's the place you're going to implement and apply Jesus' teaching on how to get what you want in Mark 11:24.

So, do you know what you want? If you don't, I believe that after you spend time in prayer and make the Word your habitation, when your heart is in a thankful state and you have praise on your lips, you'll have no problem figuring out what you truly desire.

> **Everyone is worried about you going off course with this message. That's just fear. Jesus wasn't fearful about it, so you shouldn't be either. Take off the limits!**

I'm going to pepper this book with words about releasing the fear of getting what you want and living at the top because I believe that fear is so engrained in us from centuries of bad teaching. I've seen believers who start out doing what Jesus taught and then give up out of sheer misplaced guilt and fear of standing out or going against the flow. They feel uncertain when they see the numbers of Christians who don't believe Jesus' teaching about this at all.

You can't "go with the flow" and expect to go anywhere except where everybody else is going—and if you haven't noticed, most people are living at the bottom of the barrel, and not the top! If you want to be "one of the crowd," then you may find yourself congregating near a drain hole. The path of least resistance is filled with people who wanted to go to the top, but either got distracted and gave up, or simply buckled to the pressure of those around them. God has more for you, if you want it.

So, to go to the top God's way, you have to acknowledge that you actually *have* deep desires and that Jesus has no problem whatsoever with you getting the desires of your heart so you don't have to feel guilty. You win no prizes with God by having doubt or being shy with His principles; you just lose out. You get no blue ribbon from God by holding back and not following Jesus' teaching because you'd rather seem pious to your community. God doesn't value piety that dismisses the teaching of His Son. God has so much better for you.

It's high time we all got over the fear of that word "desire" because obviously Jesus doesn't mind you having "what things soever ye desire."

THE CHURCH DOESN'T TRUST YOU, SO YOU'RE GOING TO HAVE TO TRUST YOURSELF

Most church people will tell you that "what you want" has nothing to do with the will of God, but that's just because they have believed lies and, let's face it, they don't trust you with riches or abundance or anything like that. They don't even really trust themselves! That's churchy religion and it has nothing to do with freedom in Christ. They just don't want you having "too much." Why? Fear.

Listen to me. I'm tired of fear running the church when faith and love should run the church. I'm tired of believers being poor—spiritually poor, physically poor, financially poor, and poor in every other way. Poverty is a curse! There is no lack in Heaven and I'm tired of the devil—and I believe that's where it comes from—lying and even getting good, well-meaning church people to propagate lies about God!

I do not serve a God who wants to keep His children in chains. Sin nature in the earth changed things from abundance to lack. I serve a God who sent His Son to teach all of humanity that we can have life and have it in abundance.

God sent Jesus to give us a heads up that God isn't the One trying to hold you back and hurt you. It's the devil who comes to steal, kill, and destroy people.

Stop making the mistake of believing every lie the devil throws to discredit God. Stop letting your brain spin in doubt about God's goodness and realize the bottom line is that you have authority over the devil and all his works. Choose to be on God's side.

Remember that Jesus never told you to focus on the devil and all his works, Jesus hardly bothered with the boy! In fact, even during temptation, He gave that idiot short and to the point rebuttals, and that's when the devil was straight up in His face!

Whatever you focus on has your attention, and if it's the devil all the time, that means you're going against what the Bible teaches. Jesus taught us to talk to God, to talk to the problems, to renew our mind and transform our thinking with the truth. This means turning our focus onto what is good for us, and the devil and all his works aren't good for us! The more we get ourselves in line with the truth and in line with what is good, pure, lovely, and just and choose to think on these things instead of the evil things, the better off we will be.

The more we release the fear of heart desires and having what we want, the closer we'll be to getting what we want and the happier we will be because our mind isn't in turmoil, struggling over the lie that says we *shouldn't* have what we want. Let that sink in.

> **I'm tired of the devil using religion! I'm tired of him beating people, squashing them down, stomping their hopes and dreams. I'm tired of him misusing the Word and deceiving the church into accepting the lie.**

I'm tired of good people in the church just going along with the devil's lie because they live in fear of somebody going "overboard" and "getting greedy." Well, guess what? It's not our place to be somebody else's God!

We need to trust God, yes, but we also need to trust others to live their own Christian walk and we most certainly need to start trusting ourselves! YOU are not a greedy person. You just want what your Father sent His Son to give—abundance in every area, a full life and Heaven, too. You just want to be a blessing to somebody. This is a good thing and God trusts you, so, trust yourself.

This fearlessness about the teachings of Jesus needs to come up and out of you. That's how you're going to start living at the top! It needs to come out of your heart and mouth, and then, it will begin manifesting in your life day by day, month by month, and year by year. You will move toward what God has for you.

I believe you will see yourself stand up to the mountain and speak without doubting when you are ready; that's how you're going to get rid of some things and bring new things into your life, Christ's way. You will have whatsoever things you desire when you pray, if you believe that you receive them *when* you pray. Glory to God!

I REFUSE TO APOLOGIZE FOR THE BLESSINGS OF GOD

When people criticize me for having an airplane, or a house, or a suit, or whatever tangible blessings they see on my life and ministry, I don't get mad at them or attack them over it. Why? Because I know it's coming—God's Word says so! Mark 10:30 tells me that the principle of the hundredfold works and if I receive it in this lifetime, it will come with persecution. That's right. Abundance comes with persecution. So don't expect everyone to be happy for you.

That's the reason I don't get mad at critics and want to strike back at them; I am prepared to take the heat for the blessings of God. I'm not prepared to give up what the Word says and what I believe just because *they* don't believe it or want it. Now, I don't have more faith than you, but I have established in myself that God can't lie. His Word is first place in my life. I refuse to lend my thoughts to the devil and all his works. My focus is on Jesus Christ and Him crucified.

> **When I receive something nice and people are**
> **critical of it, I just know that I cannot let it get to**
> **me and I don't need to apologize for the blessings of**
> **God. He freely gives to those who believe.**
> **If they don't want to believe or receive,**
> **they don't have to. Each of us chooses what we will**
> **and will not believe and do.**

People are always looking at me and questioning me. Sometimes I'm in a store and I can see them peering over wondering, "What's he buying? How much is he paying for that? He doesn't need that!" I can see the irritation on their faces and the judgment in their questions. I always think, *You don't know what I need; you have no concept of what I need or desire. You know nothing about me and it's amazing how you've just become an expert on nothing!* I don't mean to be rude but I've established in my heart that God can't lie and that's the end of it! They can get as mad as they want, I do not care. I wish it wasn't that way, but the Word says I'm going to get persecuted for the hundredfold and so I expect to get criticized for living at the top. That's just part of it. You should expect it, too. Don't let the judgment of others determine what you are going to do with Christ's teaching. Living at the top is for you and when you pray, you can have what you desire if you believe that you receive it. Jesus isn't wrong and God is on your side!

CHAPTER 10

~

Living at the Top Shouldn't Change Who You Are

God gave you an incredibly unique personality—you are you, and it's wonderful. It's good. You don't have to change just because you get blessed! Abundance doesn't determine who you are. Christ's Spirit within you will bring out the best of who you already are. His teaching will shift you to a place of desiring to be your "best self"—best in thoughts, words, and actions. It's all through Jesus. He is the vine, you are the branch. The connection with Him is what has the power to help you to be your "best self," prosperous in every way, but that prosperity doesn't change who you are.

You are you. There's nothing wrong with who you *are*. Life and our choices as well as the choices of others may shift and change how you think and how you act, but you are God's creation. He loves you for you. All prosperity does is add icing to your cake, so to speak.

I like that Jesus compared salvation to being born "again." He didn't cut down the first birth; He instituted the second. What needs saving is what we've become as a result of living in the saturation of this sin-sick world.

If sin hadn't entered the world at all, prosperity would be the norm. There would be no working and toiling by the sweat of our brow to get whatever we can get…no, this world was easy. That's why it seems so hard now.

We were not really meant to field the kind of sin that pervades the world today. It's made most people hobble along in life. Jesus changes all of that. Through Him, we gain redemption for our soul when we accept His sacrifice and allow Him to come into our lives. We also gain healing for our mind day by day, as we walk out our new life in Christ by spending time with Him in prayer, learning from His holy Word, and focusing on what we were always meant to be.

Jesus helps us to bust through the damaging effects of sin that have come not only because of what we've done, but also because of the effect of others on us. People closest to you may have directly or inadvertently harmed you; their choices in life had an effect on you. Sometimes, it's like collateral damage! Put that together with this sick world and its problems, along with your own bad choices, and many people end up as lost as a goose in the fog. Or, as Jesus put it in Matthew 9:36, like *"sheep having no shepherd."* Jesus is the Good Shepherd and He's not just leading us to salvation, although that would have been good. He's leading us in every area we will allow, and that is what makes life great and abundant. Christ's "born again" words are about accepting His sacrifice and realigning with the One who made you just right—the Source of everything: God!

If you don't like the way you were born, I always say, "Try it again!" I know that you are likely a believer already (and if not, I've put a salvation prayer at the end of this book), but we all need reminding that until the day we go home to be with Jesus, He is still the Potter and we are still the clay. His process of molding is to bring us to a place of fullness, to bring us back to who God created us to be before the world took its toll. It's a daily renewing of the mind that brings you closer and closer to top-level living—spiritually, physically, financially, or in any area where you apply the Word of God. Bit by bit and sometimes huge chunk by chunk (depending on what we allow), the Holy Spirit can help us to let go of all the useless junk that has been collecting. He helps us to let all that mental garbage simply fall away so that we can think His way and truly prosper.

You see, your soul (which is your mind, will, and emotions), will prosper first. *"Beloved, I wish above all things that thou mayest prosper and be in health, even as thy soul prospers"* (3 John 2). So ask yourself, what is a prosperous mind like? What does it mean to have a prosperous will? Prosperous emotions? Your spirit has already been recreated—it's perfect. It's your mind that you need to renew daily.

I Like What I Like and I'll Eat Where I Want Prosperity Will Not Change Me

People get mad at me over the fact that God has blessed me. Then, they get to know me and say things like, "You know, that guy is wealthy, but you'd never know it unless you look at his watch or his jewelry; he doesn't look like he has much of anything."

This shows me that people have a wrong idea about what it means to live at the top financially. Most see wealth as something outside of themselves, as something for "other people" and not them. Let me tell you something, as long as you see being rich as "for somebody else," it will always be just that.

They also think that being rich should look a certain way, too. In fact, whenever somebody tells me that I'm "normal" (as if they are surprised), I think, *Well, what did you expect? You must think that money alone can really change a person.* Money changes a fool who didn't know who he was in the first place. But I know who I am in Christ.

Do you ever see some of those people on television who win the lottery and flat lose their mind? Their marriages break up, there is fighting all through the family, and before they even know it, the money is gone too. Do you ever wonder why?

Proverbs 1:32 tells us that, *"The prosperity of fools shall destroy them."* So, prosperity does not destroy everyone—just fools. Wise people have no problem handling abundance.

How do you get wise? By renewing your mind to the Word of God. That's how you line up with the One who wants the best for you; get blessed and not go crazy because you don't know what to do or how to act.

The reality is that you don't have to change a thing when you are materially rich if you don't want to. Money is not your master if you are a believer. Jesus is Lord, not money! Don't make money itself something it should never be. And don't worry about how it may change you. You don't have to buy everything you see and eat what you don't even like.

Prosperity won't force you to like different things. You can do what you want with your money, and that means live where you want, eat what you want, drive what you want, etc. You don't have to suddenly look down on others because you have more. In fact, that is totally and completely at odds against God. Haughtiness is not His will. So don't get puffed up when God blesses you. Keep your heart in the right place always.

Right now, at the writing of this book, I drive a black Dodge pickup truck. It's not the best one they make, but I don't care. Why? Because I like this one! Now, I don't pick up anything in my pickup. I don't even carry people, except Cathy sometimes. I don't have a backseat because I don't want one. I could own a Rolls Royce and maybe one day I will, who knows? I can do whatever I want with my money. But wealth itself hasn't changed what I like just beause I have it. I buy what I want and not what somebody else thinks I ought to have, and that goes both ways. It's nobody's business but God's and mine…and Cathy's! So we eat where we like to eat and it's not often fancy because material blessings haven't changed our taste buds!

I'm Cajun and I like this restaurant in my area called The Seafood Pot, because Cajun French people like me enjoy boiled crawfish, boiled crabs, fried oysters, and catfish. They have these little fried creamed corn balls that my wife just loves. She has no shame clearing out a basket of them in no time flat. This is a small local place down the street from where I live. It's nothing fancy, but very delicious!

Now, people in my neighborhood see me eating there all the time and they know who I am. They know I live in a large house and sometimes they are just amazed to see me eating crawfish with the "regular" people. I don't understand this—all Cajuns love crawfish! And the ones who don't, we don't trust! I'm the same man now that I'm rich that I was when I was poor. The money hasn't changed me. I've just bought some things because I've already been giving away many things and sowing many seeds.

THE HIGH VALUE OF A "MITE"

I started sowing seeds into the lives of others, to the church and to people God put on my heart, when I was nearly broke. I've been a tither and a giver since I got born again, and I did it when it wasn't easy, when it was a sacrifice.

You see, living at the top financially doesn't mean what you may think it means. Money is a blessing and it brings a level of freedom. It opens doors for you to bless others too, which is really, after it's all said and done, the most wonderful part about prosperity. You don't realize this while you're aiming for God's best for you financially, but I promise you that it is more blessed to give than to receive. But you have to start giving when you have little in order to get to a place where you can give much.

For many people, it's harder to give a chicken leg when they only have a few. It's easier for them to give when they have abundance. But God shows us in His Word that we should give even when we are at the tiny stages. Small beginnings are precious to the Lord. That's why the widow's mite is such a heart-level, powerful teaching. Jesus saw that woman honoring God by giving from a place of need and He counted her seed as more than anyone else's at the temple that day. If He only wanted you to give out of abundance, He never would have pointed out the widow and her mites. Man looks on the outward appearance, but God looks on the heart (1 Samuel 16:7).

I believe in seedtime and harvest and I was a "widow's mite" kind of giver for many years, but I didn't stay in that state. I kept sowing and God caused me to reap. I sowed more, and He caused me to reap more. I kept growing, learning, putting my faith out there for God's best in my life—spiritually, physically, and financially—and I shut my ears as best as I could to the naysayers. The world is full of them! But I wasn't about to let them steal the truth out of my heart, so I made a choice to live at the top while I was still, in fact, on the bottom!

You need to start seeing that abundance is within your reach right now, right where you are in life. You need to see it as attainable. And you must feel comfortable within yourself knowing that you don't have to let prosperity take you for a ride. It doesn't change who you are, if you know who you are. It doesn't force you to drive a car you don't even really like or put food in your mouth that you don't care for much. No, it is a blessing from God that helps you be a greater blessing to your family and families around the world. Money with a mission is just wonderful!

You can have what you say. Those mountains will move! Your faith will work and your life will change to the degree that you choose. God wants the best for you. When you see that His best is something you can have and it's nothing to fear, it's going to set your mind free.

I'VE DECIDED TO TAKE THE HEAT

I never make an excuse for the blessings of God on my life. No way! I know that I couldn't have done any of it on my own—I'm not that good. But with God, all things are possible! God opens the doors no man can shut. He honors His Word, if I have faith in Him. He loves me, but God doesn't love me any more than He loves you. God is not a respecter of persons, but He is a respecter of faith. People may criticize me, but I've built my life around pleasing God, not people—I put Him first.

I'm a blessed man. People may not like that I enjoy jewelry, but I've always liked shiny stuff. My nickname as a kid was raccoon in Cajun French, because raccoons like shiny things. You can give them two silver coins and they will play with them for hours. Guess what? God doesn't have a problem with jewelry. He doesn't have one single issue with a fine gold watch. Why? Because precious metals aren't only on earth, they are in Heaven too! Obviously God must like pretty things, too. He likes every element He created.

Gold is in the Bible. Gold is in Heaven, too. Don't flinch when you read words like "gold, silver, onyx, jasper, and beryl"—Heaven uses all that and more for foundations, streets, and basically city and home construction. God likes it all. Everything He created is good.

Gold is concrete in Heaven and that fact doesn't make gold worthless, unless you are calling God's home and your future home worthless. No, it makes it precious to God. God does not make junk. Man makes junk.

So why are people mad at me over a little gold? It's not easy being criticized for the blessings of God. It's tough. Somebody's always looking at me weird, unless I buy them something. Then, their opinion suddenly shifts. I become a "good guy" suddenly. Isn't that sad? But, that's part of it. The Word says that if I believe for the hundredfold return I'll get it, but with persecution. So if you believe for blessings too, expect to take the heat.

I've decided that I'll take the heat. I'll be who God says I can be and have what God says I can have and I'm not going to let the devil or fearful people crush my blessings or my mind because they don't like what God said. What you see today in my life is the result of growth—not greed. It's the result of my soul prospering since 1974 when I asked Jesus to come into my life. Glory!

What You Can "See" When You Look in Your Wallet Matters

I've been poor and I've been rich—rich is better. It doesn't make you happy, but you can be comfortable in your misery. That's a joke, but it's also true for many people. Today, I don't think like a poor man. Why? Because I've already been poor and I didn't like it!

I looked to God and His Word to see how my life could be different. The Word of God lifted my mind out of poverty—spiritually, physically, financially, and in other ways too. You see, for years I looked at an empty wallet and "saw" it full. Why? Because Romans 4:17 says if I don't like what I "see" then I can change it—and so I did. Abraham was full of faith because He did what God did with His mind and with His mouth. He spoke the future into existence.

> "...calleth those things which be not as though they were."

> Romans 4:17

So, if you don't like something, change it. Change it with the words of your mouth. Now, again, the only way this works is if you have established in yourself that God can't lie. Your heart must line up with your mouth.

I can often tell when people have not established in themselves that God can't lie. They keep asking, "How long is this going to take?" They say things like, "I don't believe in that faith stuff," or, "I don't believe in naming it and claiming it." They have somehow bought into the lie that Christianity is no longer supernatural, but is now only acceptable by natural standards and reasoning. These kinds of people will make fun of you for doing what Abraham did. They will scorn what Jesus taught in favor of what they consider more "balanced." Jesus was not balanced between faith and doubt—He was fully invested and established in the truth that God can't lie! When people criticize you for speaking by faith and not by sight, for calling those things that be not as though they were, just realize that you are listening to someone who is more concerned with keeping tradition than keeping the faith.

Manifesting has nothing to do with time. The reality is that you are going to see everything come to pass, and whether it's in this lifetime or eternity is irrelevant. You are going to live forever. This is the supernatural truth about your soul. Try to grasp the timelessness of yourself and realize that you will really never die—your body may pass away but you aren't passing away. That's it. So forget about time!

The truth is that once you forget time, time forgets you and the manifestations of your faith actually come much more quickly. Why? You've eliminated one of the major doubt factors that hinder your growth. You have opted out of a fixation upon time, this life, and the fear that you will lose if you don't get it quickly enough. That fear shows a limited view of God and your own life. Your soul will live forever.

THIS LIFE CAN BE WHATEVER YOU WANT IT TO BE

God made you very powerful. What you choose to allow or to direct makes a huge difference on your life here on earth. The amount of godly success you will experience will be determined by the thoughts in your head, the words of your mouth, the motives of your heart, and the actions you take in your daily life.

The more you have doubt, the less you'll see God do in your life. The more you do what Abraham did and have faith in God by using your mouth to speak the end result, the more you'll see God do in your life because it's faith in God and yourself that does the work! You'll get things more quickly.

When you know that God will perform His Word, you can look at an empty wallet and instead of seeing an abundance of lack, you can actually see yourself living in the blessing. This is not denial. This is called changing what you "see" by faith—by calling those things which be not as though they were. This is not my opinion; this is the Word of the living God.

Seeing the life you want puts you in position to receive the life you want. This is not positive thinking, although the concept also works. This is going back to the forefathers of our faith and seeing what the Scripture says they did and taught in order for us to have the life we desire in God.

CHAPTER 11

◡

Fearlessly Embrace Your Faith Don't Be Afraid to Tell Others What God Has Done

Telling others what you believe, what God has already done for you, or what you are believing Him for in the future, is not arrogance. It's not bragging. It's simply embracing and sharing His goodness towards you. It's siding with God's Word instead of being shameful and quiet to avoid the backlash of public opinion.

Something amazing happens when you stop being fearful of the backlash. You gain peace of mind when you have faith in God and when you are brave enough to talk about it! Your stability doesn't have to be contingent upon whether other people agree or disagree with your faith. Your peace of mind doesn't have to be contingent upon whether other people like or dislike your success or desire for success in whatever area you choose to apply your faith.

It's freeing to release yourself from the fear of what others might think. It means you don't have to hide the blessings of God on your life. You can say what you want knowing that you aren't greedy—you've grown. You aren't arrogant—you're grateful to God. You aren't bragging—you are bringing glory to the One who has moved on your behalf. This is a revolutionary way of looking at the blessings of God in your life because it steps outside of the fear of man.

Fear of being condemned makes people shrink from talking about the blessings of God on their life. They fear what others will think or say about them in a negative way, so they clam up.

There is a fear of leaving others behind that is often at the root of non-success. I bust this straight in the head in my own life by deliberately talking about the blessings God has given me and about the goals I have for the future. I forced myself out of that fear of others a long time ago, and I am so free that I will never go back. Fear is bondage. It's not for me!

They're Not Really Cutting You Down
It's the Truth That They Fear and Hate

People are social. People have internal rules that they follow, and they really dislike when someone stops following the group's rules. But I'm not a bird in a flock that must follow the other birds. I'm a creation of God, created to follow my Father and not fly south when He says fly north! That's a joke, but you get my point.

Embracing your faith when it comes to the opinions of others requires fearless solidarity. At some point, you just care more about what God says than what other people say. You embrace what you've established and you can't help but tell others what God has done and what God is going to do in your life. When they cut you down for it, you can weather it because you already know that God can't lie and they just don't like that you are breaking out of religious conformity.

**The attack isn't about *you*. It's about God.
It's about Abraham. It's about Jesus. It's about
going outside of traditional rules and following your
destiny by following God's plan for your success in
this life and the next.**

So if they hate your gold, they also hate Heaven's streets. If they hate that you are speaking to your mountains and talking to your future, drawing it to you with fearless faith, guess what? They just hate the teachings of Jesus Christ. If Abraham was standing right beside them, they'd criticize him, too. Let that roll off of you like water off a duck's back.

If they hate your ability to have joy and peace of mind in the midst of being criticized, what they really hate is that you have opted out of conforming to fear. They are in fear. They follow the hidden rule of say nothing about their faith or blessings. They hate that you've broken stride. They hate that you refuse to run away.

Be Loving, Be Merciful, and Don't Let People Ruin Your Day

People will try and cut your future away by getting you angry or into strife over godly things and this blows my mind, but it's true. Good Christian people will often try and temper your faith for future good things. Again, they might love God, but they don't want you to break their hidden rule. Be merciful with them. Be loving. Do not fall into the bad habit of fighting with people.

Jesus was loving and compassionate, but He was strong in faith and He did not allow even very intimidating people like the religious hierarchy to stop Him from talking about and doing the will of His Father. Jesus didn't mind mentioning mansions in Heaven any more than He minded mentioning sin, health, love, mercy, grace, patience, glory, and power. Why? Because He had no fear of people in Him. He knew that what He had and what He had to say was more valuable than keeping the status quo.

When you are believing for something great, don't be ashamed to say it. Don't let people ruin your day! Keep your peace and realize that God's Word and God's will and your future are more important than today's criticism.

You might be living the scripture that says, *"...having done all to stand. Stand therefore..."* (Ephesians 6:13-14). Resist the urge to resent the "standing time." Standing in faith is a powerful state of being. It builds patience and character, and it has a ricocheting effect.

People notice those who are steadfast. Some will be impressed and some will be bothered. Let neither affect your continuance of faith. Your future is more important than their criticisms.

Very few people are willing to stand for what's good and believe for God's best without wavering when others don't like it. Some call it non-conformist, but I think of Christians who stick with their faith as "God-conformists." They are doers of the Word and also talkers of the Word. They can't help but speak about what God has done.

Demonstrate Deuteronomy 8:18
Remember Who Gives You the Power to Get Wealth

You have every right to brag on God! When I tell somebody I've got something nice, I know that all I'm doing is demonstrating Deuteronomy 8:18: *"But thou shalt remember the Lord thy God: for it is He that giveth thee power to get wealth, that He may establish His covenant which He sware unto thy fathers, as it is this day."*

To "remember the Lord" in relation to wealth is to honor God as the Source of your wealth. When you are blessed materially in any area, and you acknowledge that it was by God's power that you became blessed, you bring glory to His name. Everything good is from above.

Why would God give you power to get wealth if wealth itself was not good for you? Why would He say "by His stripes ye were healed" if healing was not for you? Why would He be bruised for your iniquity or have the chastisement of peace be upon Him, if redemption and peace were not good for you?

> **Everything that God offers is good for you—
> and you can feel free to brag on God because
> that's just another form of praise.
> It's praise that others can hear.**

Do you know what the tradition of the church says about wealth? They say "it's not for today" when it comes to anything tangible; they have completely abandoned the here and now life for the ever-after eternity. Why? Because they have used personal experience to validate God.

Embrace the "Impossibility" of a Miraculous God
All Things Are Possible to Them that Believe

They don't believe in prosperity because they live in lack. They don't believe in healing, because they live with sickness. They don't believe in answered prayer because they think theirs was never answered. They say things like, "You never know what God is going to do—sometimes He does, and sometimes

He doesn't." What does this mean? It means they believe in their own limited experience over the Word of God. They'd rather negate the Word to avoid what they consider inevitable disappointment.

What a sad way to think! It's just like the worldly advice, "Don't expect anything and you won't be disappointed," but that is man's way of thinking, not God's. It's not what the Word teaches us. It's a stagnant way of living that has no hope, and definitely no faith in God. In other words, they've immersed themselves in theology. Sometimes it takes a good theologian to make you misunderstand the Bible.

To live at the top, you must embrace the "impossibility" of a miraculous God. Jesus said, "With God all things are possible" and "All things are possible to them that believe." Throughout His ministry, He told people that it was "your faith" that brought forth miracles.

To embrace God's truth, you have to move beyond man's tradition. Tradition sometimes loses its passion. It gets watered down because people begin favoring what's natural over what's supernatural. Sometimes you have to remind yourself that none of us would be believers if Christ hadn't risen from the dead. Christianity is based on the supernatural.

Those fish and loaves that were miraculously increased to feed the 5000? Supernatural prosperity! That net of Peter's that didn't catch one fish all night but started breaking under the massive catch once Christ got involved? Supernatural prosperity!

Remember that Peter had toiled all night fishing and had caught nothing. But once he lent his boat to Jesus (who used it as a pulpit to preach to others), the "harvest" on that "seed" was a supernatural haul! Sowing and reaping works, and God's ways are higher than our ways.

As believers, we can't let ourselves slip back into pure natural thinking because we have been given the mind of Christ. We must be brave enough to use it. Regardless of what people who value tradition over truth say about us, we must step out in faith, and we can't be afraid to brag on God. The whole Bible is a bragging session about God! So if you chime in about what He's done for you, you are doing just fine!

To Live Future-Minded Is Fun— Dream the "End Result"

You can't let your past dictate to you what you will and will not believe; the Word must be first place in your own mind. God's will over your will. His Word over your word. I love to dream big dreams. I love to push my faith forward. I like where I've been, but I don't want to stagnate in nostalgia. There is a lost and dying world out there; my goal is to help people find Jesus, change their lives for the better, and succeed in being whatever God has called them to be. God's Word helps people be successful from the inside out, as their soul prospers. So I'm interested in teaching and preaching to the soulish realm—the mind, the will, and the emotions.

If you get your mind in order, you'll think straight. If you get your will in order, you'll do more. If you get your emotions in order, you'll live with a lot more peace. Fixating on problems instead of God's promises is like being on a treadmill of despair. Jump off and start dreaming and using your faith.

No matter what happened in your past, whether it was terrible, wonderful, or like most people, a mix of both, you can't move forward if you stay stuck in your past. Time is only moving forward and God has new things for you. Each day is an opportunity to find joy, push your faith forward, and become more of what God said you really are at your core. Everyone needs something to look forward to. It is so fun to dream and then act on those dreams.

My wife, Cathy, says, "Jesse's got so many plans." I'm future-minded. I don't worry about the problems of the future; I focus on the good that is coming my way. I think of the people I will reach with the message of Jesus, people who will be saved and healed, delivered and set free, who will totally change their lives around and succeed God's way. I think of their children who will learn to talk to God themselves, to lean on Him, to have faith and do big things for the world. I think of their children's children and how the wealth of the godly grandparents will have ripple effects helping future generations both spiritually and materially. These dreams I have are end-result dreams. What I do and what I say today has a ripple effect, the same as what you do and what you say has ripple effects.

Sometimes life gets overwhelming when we aren't full of the Spirit and when we let today's problems drag out for years in our mind. Be a futurist! Move forward! Fill your mind with what will make you smile in the future. Any time that you catch yourself worrying, give it to God in prayer. Let go where it's safe to let go, which is in His presence. Your prayer life should settle your soul and stir your heart for good things, and it should free your mind up to dream.

CHAPTER 12

*Use Your Faith and Embrace
the Good Future God Has for Your Life*

Never be afraid to let yourself dream. God gave you that mind for a reason, not to think up a disastrous future, but to imagine and use your faith for a good future, to focus on what is good for you, for your family, and for the world at large.

I believe in progression. Out of progression will come possession—this is God's way. You believe it, say it, and do what is in line with the Word, then possession comes. Patience is a part of the process. The Scripture says it was only when Abraham patiently endured that he received the promise.

It doesn't matter if it takes one day or ten years. Stand and having done all to stand, stand therefore, letting patience have it's perfect work. In the end, you will be perfect and entire, wanting nothing (James 1:4). Notice the Word went beyond saying we would need nothing, into the realm of desire. Again, want is not a bad thing.

God loves you and wants the best for you. The faith system is in place to get you there, day by day, overcoming hurdles and enjoying life in the process. The challenge itself should not overwhelm you and if it does, you know that you are doing this in your own strength, using your mind for what is not helping you at all.

Your spirit can embrace the intellect, but your intellect may rarely embrace the Spirit. Accept this and lean to the strongest part of you, the place where you were born again: in the Spirit. The Holy Spirit will connect with your spirit throughout your day, meeting you in times of need and helping you to let what is hindering your mind fall away under the strength of your own holy, recreated, saved-by-grace spirit. Let your spirit rise up and conquer as you move throughout your day, knowing that you are going somewhere. Your future is too important to squander in worry or thoughts of what did and didn't work in the past. Faith sees the future.

Your past must not dictate your future. What you are embracing in the Word and doing now is what matters.

Faith is a now thing and patience and progression are key, don't ever throw away the message of faith. The faith message is in the Word of God, even if there are people who don't like it. Abraham lived by faith. Jesus lived by faith and taught faith. So did Jesus' disciples, and so do millions around the world today.

You are never alone. In Matthew 18:19-20, Jesus said, *"Again I say unto you, That if two of you shall agree on earth as touching any thing that they shall ask, it shall be done for them of My Father which is in heaven. For where two or three are gathered together in My name, there am I in the midst of them."*

When two agree as touching anything, there is a unity of godly purpose and love, and then, God is in your midst. Consider the truth that you don't even need another human being to believe with you for God's best. Why? Because Christ has risen and sent His Holy Spirit to dwell on the earth and inside of you. The Holy Spirit is your "two" and that is enough for miracle-guidance, miracle-blessings, and miracle-possession!

I pray that you have even more people to join with you and the Holy Spirit and say, "I'll pray. I'll agree in faith with you. I'll be your 'two.' I'll 'stand and having done all to stand, stand' with you." Look for people who will lift you up in your quest for God's best, not for people who spend all their time tearing down the messages of Jesus and trying to take what's good away from God's people. This is foolish and damaging—don't be a part of it. Be a part of what's good. Faith in God is good!

Never forget that the world is full of people who want to tear down God's goodness towards His children who look for ways to doubt and tear down truth and replace it with a controlling lie. Jesus told us that He only spoke what God told Him to speak and so "the faith message" that Christ taught is from God.

> **When somebody tells me, "That faith stuff doesn't work," I think, *Well, either Jesus is lying or you are lying! I pick YOU.***

Let their hate roll off your back, don't let a word of it redirect your thoughts to what is not good. God is love, and you've been called to love even the unlovable doubters of this world. Trust God day by day. Lean on the Holy Spirit and know that living at the top is nothing if it's not faith and love! Nothing works in the spirit realm without those two things (Galatians 5:6). Faith works by love, so let it work.

There is a reason for everything. While there are many who will say, "That faith junk doesn't work," you must always remember that it took faith to save your soul. Go and see in your Bible how many times Jesus equated miracles to the person's faith. Faith is the currency God requires in order to make exchanges from the spirit world to the physical world. Abraham needed faith. Jesus needed faith. You need faith, too, to get anything out of the spirit to manifest.

CARD GAMES, GOOD FOOD, AND FAITH—I AIM TO WIN!

It makes no difference how many times you may have thought, "It didn't work." I mean, how many times have I played a card game with my friends and lost? Not many! That's a joke, but the point is that I didn't stop playing because I lost once. I'm Cajun and my wife and I play this card game called Pedro with family and friends. It's always the women against the men. We like the competition and it's fun.

Now, I know some of you don't like cards, but I'm sorry! This is my Cajun culture and there isn't one "Thou shalt not play Pedro" in the Word. Cajuns have played this game since we were kids. Now, on the off-chance, odd day that I actually lose a game, you will never catch me saying, "These cards don't work! The game is rigged!" No, there were other factors at play.

So, what do I do? I release the disappointment, remind myself of the rules, and start a new game with success on my mind. Every single time is another opportunity to win, to have patience and progress until I possess the land. I look at a losing game like maybe "somebody" (Cathy) hindered my success that time. Or maybe it was me...maybe I got distracted and didn't play as well as I could that day. Maybe I didn't stay vigilant and keep my mind in the game. Or maybe I grew weary and got up from the table before I could win and get the glory. This analogy is a joke in a way, but I hope you get the point I'm trying to make. There are many factors in why one loses or wins. I never throw away my faith.

If that analogy doesn't work, how about this one? How many times have you ordered something at a restaurant and ended up saying, "Awwww, man! I don't like this at all! Yuck!" It might have put a bad taste in your mouth, but that didn't stop you from going out and eating again. There are a lot of reasons why believers don't get what they want. The spirit world is a lot like a restaurant, and many believers try to get food without consulting the menu. Many just complain to the waiter, instead of saying what they want. If they didn't get food, it might be because they sat down at the table and never once opened their mouth. Maybe they just wished and hoped for food, and then got angry that the cook didn't bring them anything, and then said, "This doesn't work!"

Words matter—Jesus wouldn't have told you to "say to the mountain" if speaking wasn't part of the process of faith. Put in your order! Faith speaks and expects the food to come, knowing that the cook is God and He's faithful to deliver what He promises in the Word.

Maybe you opened the menu of the Word and didn't ask for what you desired in your heart; maybe you shrunk back in fear and doubted that you could have it or that God even wanted you to have it, even though He put it on the menu. Then, when you didn't get what you desired, you got a little upset.

> **Faith doesn't work if you don't look at the menu. How can you know what's available? Faith doesn't work if your mouth is asking for one thing but your heart wants another. Your heart and mind need to be on the same page.**

God will not agree with your confusion. He won't do it! You'll starve while He waits for you to decide. Remember, you can't get what you don't know that you want. And you can't get what you don't ask for. The door will never be opened if you don't knock. This spirit world is built on words and faith. The natural world is built on words and actions. They both make waves in different ways that create change, and you live in both places, so you need to function in both well. The Holy Spirit will help you.

THE WORD IS DESIGNED TO DISCERN YOUR HEART

I've never been the type of person who has trouble knowing what he wants. I find it easy to know, and I go about the process of implementing what I want to produce both in the spirit and in the natural.

Not everybody is this way. Some people spin and don't really know what they want. In other words, they don't know what is in their heart, so they feel unsettled. If you find yourself not knowing what is in your own heart, here is what to do. Turn to the Word. Hebrews 4:12 gives great insight into the heart of man: *"For the word of God is quick, and powerful, and sharper than any twoedged sword, piercing even to the dividing asunder of soul and spirit, and of the joints and marrow, and is a discerner of the thoughts and intents of the heart."*

**The Word of God can divide your *SOUL*
(mind, will, and emotions) from your *SPIRIT*
(the part of you that is perfectly in tune with God).
The Word of God is a discerner of the
thoughts and intents of your heart.**

So, who needs this information most? YOU. You are the one who needs to know and God is the One who will reveal it to you. God put desires in your heart for a reason, so don't go through life ignoring what will bring you the most satisfaction and joy. Your destiny will be produced in reality by walking out the desires of your recreated, born again heart.

The Holy Spirit helps you rightly divide the Word of truth on a personal level, exposing thoughts of the mind that need to go and showing you the innermost thoughts and intentions of your heart, the things that need to stay, fill your mind, and become goals for the moment, for the day and for your future.

Remember that the devil is the author of all confusion, so confusion is not for you. Double-mindedness brings instability in every way. Clarity comes when the heart and mind are on the same page. If you've been ignoring your heart, you might be surprised at just what is revealed when you meditate on the Word and let the Holy Spirit lead you. He will create a clean heart and renew a right spirit in you like Psalm 51:10 says, so let Him do His work. And, if your heart is troubled, give those troubles to the One who is capable of hearing them, doing something about them, and settling your soul.

Prayer is not escape. It's communion with your Father; it's the building of a relationship. Let your Father, through His Words and His Spirit, teach you and show you what you need to see inside of yourself when it comes to desires. Then, speak!

God is proud of you. He wants to hear you talk to that mountain. I believe it blesses God when we throw off the shackles of daily life and focus on why we are here and what we are going to do with the precious life He gave us. I think He likes it when we tell that mountain where to go!

I think God loves to see us say what we desire. We are following in His footsteps when we do. The Word says that He created the world and mankind by the words of His mouth. I believe it brings Him joy to see us follow His lead, imitating Him like dear children by *speaking* in faith, doing what He did and creating *something* from what looks like *nothing*!

So let your words and your prayers be known to God and to the air around you. Let your prayer be with "present" faith and not "future" faith. Everything is available in the spirit and you are a speaking spirit. You will have in the natural what you first speak in the spirit. It is yours, in Jesus' name!

CHAPTER 13

The Magnetism of Faith— Expect Company, Living at the Top Is Magnetic to Others

When you begin living at the top, your faith will begin to attract others who want what you have: love, joy, hope, wisdom, health, wealth, good relationships, and all the rest. Faith is magnetic and it's a powerful source of personal strength in the world. It's power with no guile or will to harm attached to it; a light in the darkness that can't be put out.

A very rich, successful man with a heart for God, like Abraham, can do a lot more for the world than a successful man like Lot, who was less interested in following God and more interested in pitching his tent toward Sodom. Like Abraham, your gold, your silver, and your material possessions won't be simply markers of your "success," they will become a testament to many around you that the hand of God is on you and that your faith in God works. This is magnetic to people who are also interested in living at the top.

Believers who are truly living at the top, both spiritually and financially, are interested in making the world a better place and their money and possessions become a useful tool to establish God's covenant on the earth. His covenant is love and mercy towards people through Jesus Christ, who taught that all people could gain not only eternal life in Heaven through acceptance of Him as Savior, but also an abundant life here on earth by following the principles of the Bible.

This life is a vapor and many believers know that God blesses them so that they might be a blessing to others. We are conduits of His Spirit and distribution houses of His blessings, sharing with others the truth about God's love for the world and using our finances to make this world better.

> **I like the term "money with a mission" because a wealthy believer who loves God enjoys making his money work for the good of people.**
> **There is a lot to do in the world, and there is no shortage of money to do it.**

A lot of ungodly people do not care one bit about this world; they only care what they can get out of it. Many actually work directly against God, making the world a terrible place for as many as they can. God-fearing people do the opposite, which is why we need more believers to be serious about gaining wealth and sharing the Gospel.

We are the Goliath slayers. We are the Daniels. Everyone around us knows that we follow God. We are the water-walking disciples who do the impossible; we look to Jesus and aren't afraid to get out of the boat of religion and walk out on that water in faith. We are kings and priests on this earth. Our leadership is seen everywhere we go. It affects those who are attracted to our faith in God and our success as followers of His Word.

THE TRICKLE-DOWN EFFECT OF LEADERSHIP

Leaders have a profound effect on those they are leading. I'm an evangelist and, at the writing of this book, have been preaching as a guest speaker in churches across America and the world for over thirty-eight years. I can tell you that in any given church, I've found that the faithful in that congregation are the direct result of their leader.

If the pastor is sad, most of his people will begin to live out that sadness as well. You'll hear a lot of despondent talk in that church. There will be very little anger or action because sadness is debilitating; hope is what gives people the energy to move. Confidence of any kind in what God can do or will do is buried under words like, "Well, you know how God is…sometimes He does and sometimes He doesn't. He probably won't this time, but I'll pray and give it a shot."

If a pastor is sick, he will often preach out of that lack of health. He might cast a good light on sickness and even preach that infirmity is God's way of "trying to teach you something." Never mind that there is no sickness in Heaven. Never mind that healing was what Jesus did in His earthly ministry. Never mind that Jesus never once laid His hand on someone and *gave* them disease. Never mind that "by His stripes ye were healed" is part of the blood covenant. No, the pastor will preach His experience instead of the Scripture, and his people will follow his lead. They "calleth those things that be not as though they were" until they are, and the sickness in that church will be as natural and free-flowing as a branch flowing downstream. Those people usually really like talking about their every ailment and showing their scars and the local hospitals make a lot of money in the process!

If a pastor is financially broke, he will usually preach from that place of lack as well and, consequently, most of his people will find themselves thinking and speaking through a lens of "never enough" or "Look at them, they have too much." The people will make an excuse for poverty or even preach that it's a good thing. They usually resent prosperity and only preach about "spiritual riches." Never mind that the earth was created with an overflow of material abundance or that it's only man's inhumanity to man that starves people. Never mind that the Word tells us God was the One who caused Solomon to become the richest person who ever lived because he cared more about people than power, or that an old man named Abraham followed God and was made very rich in the process. None of that matters because lack has clouded the vision of that church, and all those unmet desires make the people flat mad. They think, "Somebody's got to pay!" So, you'll hear a lot of envy. You'll hear clear resentment towards wealthy people and a hatred of any sermon on prosperity. You'll also see them flinch if you talk too much about money.

There is a trickle-down effect from leader to people. We are all affected by the words that we repetitively hear, by the churches and ministries we give our attention to.

Be aware of who you hear repetitively.
Be aware of what you are consistently saying.
Don't let personal experience be the foggy lens that
you see through—look through the eyes of your
faith in God and let His Word be the basis
for what comes out of your mouth.

You are a leader and you need to both hear good words and give good words. The words you choose to repetitively hear are either building you up or tearing you down, choose to hear good words. The words you say repetitively are heard by others; choose to say good words. This world is hard enough and God has a plan for all of us. You are a leader and every day you choose the words that will affect people around you for better or for worse; choose what's better. People need it. You need it. Stir up the gift of God within you and give what you have inside of you to change the atmosphere and make things better than they were when you showed up.

LEADERS CHARGE THE ATMOSPHERE

Have you ever walked into a room where a couple was fighting just moments earlier? Isn't it weird that you can "feel" the irritation or frustration in the air? They don't have to say a word.

People charge the atmosphere. Even if you say nothing, never forget that what is inside of you is coming out into the atmosphere around you. You are a spirit being and the condition of your soul (mind, will, emotions) has an effect on everyone you come into contact with. This is yet one more reason why you should sow good words into yourself. Sow the holy Word of God.

The Holy Spirit lives within you, and the joy of the Lord is your strength. Move in the direction of joy. Move in the direction of peace and prosperity of all kinds. Don't put a cap on what God can do. Don't limit God with your own thoughts, much less your words! He is limitless. Never look at someone and think so lowly of them that you have no hope to give. There is always hope. As long as there is a breath in the body, that person needs hope and love.

Realize that your very thoughts create an atmosphere before you even open your mouth. Do you realize this? As a man thinketh, so is he (Proverbs 23:7).

**Your thoughts aren't just creating your reality—
they are affecting everybody else's!
Think of your thoughts like sound waves.
Music creates waves. Let your thoughts be like
a silent music that soothes people,
energizes people, and uplifts people.**

Let the words of your mouth and the meditations of your heart be pleasing to God, because they will also be pleasing to you and to others who are attracted to you (Psalm 19:14).

You are the leader in your own life. Accept that if you want to live at the top, you just may also be a leader of others. Leaders charge the atmosphere with direction. It's as if their "waves" are more focused than others and they lead not only by words, but by sheer strength of character. Let your good character speak even before you do. Let your presence bring waves of good into the room.

IMPLEMENT AND APPLY—YOU WILL ATTRACT

Once I established in myself that God can't lie and once I began embracing others in what I had already established in myself, I noticed something change in my life. It was as if people were drawn to me like a magnet. What I had, people wanted. They saw different things in me than what I even saw in myself. I just knew that I believed God more than I believed circumstances, and because of that, circumstances vastly changed in my life.

When you embrace others in what you've already established in yourself—your faith in God, your strength of spirit, your joy for living without religious limitations, and with a full desire for God's will and your destiny to be fulfilled—people will be attracted to you. Those who want to live at the top will find you, ask you questions, want your friendship, and look to you as someone with wisdom in how the world works.

I'm a very busy man. I've got a lot that I want to do, projects God has given me in order to reach more people and change more lives with the Gospel and the principles of the Word. I write books like this and speak all over the world to share what God has given me so that others can live the life God gave them in a limitless way.

When I teach prosperity, it's because I know what it's like to be poor. I know that God can fix poverty in a person's life if they'll follow Him. The Holy Spirit within them is brilliant and powerful. The Word at their fingertips is priceless. Their faith in God and in themselves is astronomically important. They can change their own situations and the world around them.

Yet some people think all I want to do is control them, but nothing could be further from the truth. I've got enough going on! I certainly don't need or want to control another human being—that's too much work. My work is helping people, not controlling people. The only thing I need to control is my own flesh. That's daily, not just Sunday! I have to crucify my own flesh so that I can implement and apply the Word. I have to crucify my own flesh so that I keep moving forward in my destiny, so that I reach my destination and help others reach theirs. It has nothing whatsoever to do with control. I can't even control my wife, Cathy! When I was a teenager, my daddy would say, "Boy, I may be the head of this house, but I ain't the boss! Don't get me in trouble. Ask ya Mama!"

All of us are just called to be God's best of who we are—and His best is abundance! It's living at the top! That attracts others. Make sure that you treat that attraction with zero control.

Don't let your flesh take you for a ride; you must love the people and not the power. You must realize that the only thing you control is you. The rest is a continual filling up and flowing out of your wisdom, your knowledge, and your faith in God. Don't let the devil stroke your ego! Many people let power over other people go to their heads and ruin life for them and everybody they influence.

Jesus was not a control-freak. Abraham was not a control-freak. You shouldn't be a control-freak either. When you lead others, you have power. Be superior to power, and not driven by it. Realize that everyone has free will and people can stop listening at any time. And if you become power hungry and controlling, they should stop listening! Everyone has free will. This is a gift from God. Leaders should lead out of a mindset of care, protection, and love for those they are over.

God Doesn't Respond to Begging

Too many people pray without considering the way God created this world to work. They say things like, "Lord, do You see this sickness? This lack? This anxiety? This problem?" I may shock you when I share this, but God doesn't respond to begging. You might not like that, but it's the way it is.

God responds to faith—He always has, He always will, and no matter what you say or do, you won't change the laws of faith. He may answer your question and say, "I don't deal with that—you deal with that. My Son already took care of that on the cross. Now, you must believe. You must receive. You must hear My Word and accept what I already gave you."

You won't live at the top if you waste your breath pleading and begging God for something He already said in His Word is yours. Begging changes nothing. Faith changes everything. Hearing the Word brings faith.

Prayer brings safety and solace, pure energy with the Father, and for lack of a better word, it "enlarges" His Holy Spirit inside of you. Prayer is a time of power-sourcing. Build up your faith in Him and what He has already done; it will dislodge the fear and move you to the top.

Say What You Want, Not What You Have

One of the most common mistakes I see Christians make when they pray or even talk to each other about material things is this: They say what they *have* instead of what they *want*. I've even seen really good leaders slip back into the habit. It's very natural to only look at what's in front of you. But faith sees further.

Most people tell God what they *have* when they pray, but God already knows what you have. He knows where you are. He is waiting for you to speak what you *want*. Your mouth can't be full of "today" if you want something better tomorrow. Be vigilant about not filling the air with what you don't want and what you see right now in the natural.

Always stating the obvious, like "I'm broke" or "I'm so sick" or "Things are falling apart," doesn't point you anywhere. It may be a fact, but it isn't the "truth." Telling it like it is isn't wise; tell it like you want it to be, because that's speaking to the mountain. Facts about how it is now won't move mountains into the sea or bring solutions or future desires into the world. It's what you think, speak, and do that propels your future.

People get stuck sometimes when they feel overwhelmed by a present situation. It's why they do the opposite of what Jesus said and start fixating on how bad the mountain is that's blocking their view.

When all you see is the mountain itself and you feel overwhelmed, you need to consider the God you are serving. Remind yourself that you serve El Shaddai....not El Cheapo! El Shaddai is the God of more than enough. El Cheapo is the God of not enough!

God is almighty. He's abundant in every area, and He is the Source of your abundance. There is no lack in Him. In fact, just going over the names of God and what they mean can really build your faith. I've listed the names of God below to remind you. I hope these help you to back up and see the big picture of the God you serve. I encourage you to use them when you feel overwhelmed. Notice that they are confessions or affirmations. This is so you don't just read about God, but put yourself into it because making it personal helps a lot. Use these in your prayer time or anytime you are struggling with the feeling of being overwhelmed. Speak His name over yourself and your situation and just see if it doesn't help you realize how powerful the God you serve is. He loves you.

NAMES OF GOD
CONFESS HIS GREAT POWER

EL – Almighty God. You are mighty, strong, and first in my life.

ELOHIM – My Creator. You are all-knowing. The God over all the universe, all life, and all nations. The One who preserves me.

EL SHADDAI – All-sufficient, all-bountiful, Almighty God. You are the One who is more than enough, the One who takes care of me.

ADONAI – Owner of my life, the One who gives gifts and equips. I am not my own. I have been bought with a price, the blood of the Lamb. I love You and serve You. My spirit, soul, and body belong to You.

JEHOVAH – Eternal, permanent, and self-existent, the Possessor of Eternal Life. You are full of moral and spiritual attributes. It is my joy to submit to Your good ways, to always follow You.

JEHOVAH-JIREH – My Provider. You are the One who makes provision for me. You foresee all my needs and have provided redemption for me. Thank You for sending Your Son. In Christ, You always provide for me.

JEHOVAH-RAPHA – My Healer. You are the One who heals my spirit, soul, and body. You restore me. You cure me. You take all disease away from me. By the stripes on Christ's back, I am healed—spirit, soul, and body.

JEHOVAH-NISSI – My Banner. You are the One who delivers and saves me. You give me victory. You do miracles. I hold You high, like a sign for the world to see. Your Son is my banner of redemption. You always lead me in Your triumph, through Christ Jesus.

JEHOVAH-MEKADDISHKHEM – My Sanctifier. You purify me and separate me. I recognize Your statutes and I'm dedicated to You. Your Son is my High Priest, my Sanctification. I am redeemed through His shed blood. Through Christ, I am spotless and I live holy.

JEHOVAH-SHALOM – My Peace. You still my heart and soul and give me divine rest. I am wholly reconciled to You. Through Christ, You have paid my debts and my trust and obedience is to You. Jesus, the Prince of Peace, lives in me and His peace rules my heart.

JEHOVAH-TSIDKENU – My Righteousness. You are the One who always makes it right. You render justice. You declare innocence. You acquit me. You are perfect and righteous and do not overlook guilt. You measure and weigh, and You always do what's right. You have given me Jesus to take away my sin and guilt, He has paid the price for me. I'm accepted in Your sight. I'm cleansed by the blood of Christ.

JEHHOVAH-SHAMMAH – My Ever-Present God. You are always there. You never leave me or forsake me. Your fullness and glory dwells in me and around me. My purpose is to glorify You. I will enjoy Your presence today, tomorrow, and forever.

JEHOVAH-RO'I – My Shepherd. You guide me with love and correct me with kindness. You are my Companion and my Friend. You cherish me. You lead me. You instruct me and call me by my name. Jesus is my Good Shepherd, I know His voice and answer when He calls. Thank You for being with me day and night, caring for my soul. I choose to serve You and live in the shadow of Your great love.

CHAPTER 14

Shut the Door So the Oil Can Flow! Let Them Say What They Will, You Are Going to the Top!

There was a good reason why the prophet of God in 2 Kings 4:4 told the widow to "shut the door" before the miracle of the barrels being supernaturally filled with oil could begin to flow. This woman needed a miracle. She was in dire straights. Elisha noticed that there were people around who had the power to hinder what the woman needed and wanted, and he gave her strict instructions to shut the door on them.

Distractions hinder our faith, whether they come from our own mind or the people we surround ourselves with. Big mouths of doubt can really stop the flow of oil, so to speak. When you are believing for something from God, when you are using Christ's methods and speaking to the mountain in faith, remember to keep your distractions to a bare minimum.

Don't be afraid to shut the door on the ones who only speak doubt—keep those dream killers outside! Just like you shift doubt-filled thoughts out of your head, sometimes you have to shift doubt-filled people out of your room. Some people, even Christians, don't want the best for you. In fact, if they were at the widow's house that day and had been allowed to stay, jealousy would have driven them to blab doubt and even go so far as to physically try to keep the miracle from happening.

Dream killers are people who say nothing good about what you are believing for. Dream killers get mad when you get blessed. They really don't want you rising up. They don't want you going higher than they are. This is pure fear at work.

You see, when your barrel starts being filled with oil, some people will get so mad that they try and poke holes in your barrel to drain you of oil so that you can be just as miserably broke as they are. This is a sad fact and it's just as prevalent in the church as it is in the world at large. Some people will never be happy that you succeed.

You May Have to Love Some People from Afar

Success has a price and sometimes it costs you a relationship with someone who does not have your best interest at heart. It doesn't mean that you cut them totally out of your life, though you may have to do that. Some people you need to love from afar. Jesus did not remain on the cross. Jesus had only so many days that He allowed Himself to be relentlessly tortured. He only stayed in the grave for so long.

God doesn't expect you to be hit repetitively by people. You should turn the other cheek for the sake of the Gospel, but only you know when it is time to rise up, walk away, and love from afar. You cannot hold onto bitterness, or it will damage not only your mind and heart, but will also steal your future. That's why I mentioned forgiveness earlier in this book.

What you must realize is that anytime that you start rising up in life, you will create an atmosphere that puts some people in fear. People fear success much more than you think because it's an unknown. They've never been where you are going and take no comfort in your success. They only have apprehension.

Living at the top makes those who don't want to have faith or work uncomfortable because you are threatening the staus quo. You are rocking the boat. Your every success shines a light they may not want to see. You have to accept this as a fact of life and success. It's a sad truth, but it is a reality.

Many times, relationships dissolve. People get shut out of the room. It's not mean. It's not unloving. It's not petty. It's what you have to do sometimes if you want to get the oil into the barrel. If you are the widow in the situation and your children's lives depend on it, you will do what God said and stop casting your pearls before swine. Some people love mud and they always will and there is nothing you can do to force them to think otherwise. They enjoy slop!

Shut the Door on the Dream Killers

Instead of trying to convince these people or get them on your side, go into your house and shut the door and work on filling your barrel with oil through faith. Instead of talking about good things, let them see some good things. If they try and hurt you, realize that they really don't know what they are doing. Jesus said this when He was hanging from a cross, beaten by people He was dying to save.

If there are dream killers in your life that you must shut the door on, do it. If there are people who don't appreciate your pearls, don't allow them to trample what God is doing for you. Remind yourself that if only they could rise up out of the slop, they would see the beauty of what God is doing in your life. If they could put away the fear, they would see that they can rise to the top with you and the relationship would be better than it ever was before because you'd be able to do it together. If only they weren't jealous of your success, they might gain eyes clear enough to see that God is just as willing to do the exact same for them.

Love is not abusive, so feel free to close the door on those who want to do you harm. The Holy Spirit will lead you when the time is right. Don't let your love for them keep you from moving forward in life and obtaining God's best for you. Love them, but let go, because sometimes it's only when the door has been closed that the miracle oil begins to flow.

Shut the Door So the Oil Can Flow!
Let Them Say What They Will,
You Are Going to the Top!

What You Want Is at the Top of the Barrel
What You Have Is at the Bottom

Faith works in the negative as well as the positive. This is why it's so important to say what you want and not what you have if what you have is negative. Wherever you focus your faith is where your faith will go to work. If you want to live off the top of the oil-filled barrel, so to speak, then you have to fill the barrel first! You can't do that by focusing on the shortage. To fill the barrel, your faith needs to be focused on what you *want* and not on what you *have* because what you want is on the *top* of the barrel, and what you have is at the *bottom*.

Here are some examples of faith in the negative and what NOT to do if you want to "have whatsoever you say" like Jesus taught:

If your barrel is filled with lack and you keep talking about it, you are focusing on lack instead of abundance. Your faith will work to keep the barrel empty of wealth.

If your barrel is filled with sickness and you keep talking about it, you are focusing on sickness instead of health. Your faith will work to keep the barrel empty of health.

If your barrel is filled with problems and things you don't want, and you keep talking about them, your faith will work to keep your barrel empty of solutions and empty of what you desire, which is God's best.

You can't spend day and night talking about the problem and expect anything different. You'll just heap anxiety on top of your problem and the barrel will stay exactly as it is or it will get worse, because faith produces what you believe in your heart and confess with your mouth.

**If you believe lack is your destiny
and you say it, you can be sure that
lack will always be a part of your life.
This is faith working in the negative. Don't do it!**

You've got to learn to turn it around and focus your faith on what you *want* inside that barrel! Again, what you want is on the top of the barrel (abundance) and what you have is on the bottom (lack). Spiritually, physically, and financially, it is God's will for your barrel to be full and overflowing with enough for you and all the good works you want to do in this life. So, say what you want, not what you have!

Let the Detractors Squawk… They Won't Do It Forever

The world understands making money, but the church has condemned people for even desiring success. This creates an even greater uphill battle for the believer who uses his faith to fill his barrel. Godly people who are very successful have often encountered a much greater amount of resistance towards their success, at least in the beginning.

Let them squawk and call you crazy when you are working at filling the barrel. Let them attack you when they see through the crack of the closed door that oil is flowing!

It's funny how the detractors stop squawking once you fill the barrel and start living off the top of it. Those same people who cut you on the way up will turn right around and pat you on the back as if they never did anything to discourage you. They'll probably ask you for some oil, too, but that's not the point here! The point is even detractors sometimes change, once they see you go from the bottom of the barrel to the top. Sometimes they'll even come to you for advice.

In the beginning of my ministry, I was cut down so much for believing by faith. Anything I did seemed to be scrutinized and condemned, even by people I greatly admired. It was as if they didn't want me to rise in life, and they surely didn't think God could do anything with me as a preacher. They criticized my accent. It didn't matter that I was a former rock musician, Cajun from South Louisiana—they wanted me to sound like I was a Southern Baptist theologian with three points and a poem.

Later, when I was established and I would tell people what I was believing for, it was beyond what they could believe for and, again, beyond what they thought I could do. The truth was that I agreed with them about my limitations! I knew I couldn't do any of it on my own. That was the difference—they were looking at me, but I was looking at God. When you are looking at God, your barrel seems easy to fill!

They Came and Sat on My "Crazy!"

I remember telling people that I was believing to build our ministry facilities debt free and under budget. I had a model built. Nobody believed it could be done, especially the bank people who knew how much was in the account. I can remember sharing my vision and people saying, "This guy actually believes this! I don't agree with all that confession. I don't believe in that money teaching and that faith message. If he thinks he's building all that debt free, he's crazy!"

Well, later on, they came and sat inside my "crazy!" They put their big, doubtful butts right on a debt free pew! They praised the Lord and prayed right inside a debt free and under budget sanctuary. They toured a debt free and under budget TV studio, administrative buildings, and product distribution warehouse. How about that for "crazy"—as the saying goes, it can't be done until somebody does it.

I built the first church building in the greater New Orleans area that was constructed completely debt free and under budget. This is what I was told by several banks. You can't find anything on my ministry property that has a mortgage note on it. And if you think I am that good, that I can produce that much and keep producing it on my own, you are living in a dream world. This is God's doing and it is marvelous in my eyes (Psalm 118:23)!

Shut the Door So the Oil Can Flow!
Let Them Say What They Will,
You Are Going to the Top!

**God takes "crazy" faith and produces amazing
results that others look at in wonder.**

They say, "How did he do it?" and when I tell them it's
God and faith in God, they *still* don't believe it. They can walk
around in it, sit on it, and see it with their own eyes and still
they have a hard time believing the truth. That's human nature.
It's full of doubt.

Well, got past my doubts long ago; I did that when God told
me He was going to give me an airplane but I was still riding
around in a tiny Toyota. I didn't have the money to even fill up
that Toyota with gasoline sometimes, and yet God wanted me
to stretch and look into the sky to see the future He would bring
me to if I could "only believe" that all things were possible with
Him. Do you see? If you allow God, He will take you from
small beginnings and together with Him, you will get to a place
in life one day that you look back and feel utterly amazed.

**Let them call you crazy! Don't take that as a shot
against your character. One day you'll manifest
exactly what they called you crazy about.**

Just like I talked to the detractors who told me I could never
build what I built debt free and under budget, you'll be able to
say your own version of this:

"You thought I was crazy…but you're sitting on my crazy now! You're walking on my crazy now! You're driving out on my crazy now! It was crazy to you back then, but it's always been just faith in God to me. So, yes, sling your mud because God brought me from poverty to prosperity. Like Abraham, God has made me crazy blessed in every area I have faith for. I'm crazy at peace. I'm crazy healed. I'm crazy rich. I've got crazy-good relationships. I am crazy 'whatsoever' because I serve a God who can perform anything I dare to put my faith towards. It's called 'all things are possible to them that believe.' My God has been good to me!"

Glory! I just stirred myself up! I hope you are stirred up too. Don't for a moment think that this is arrogance or trying to poke somebody else in the eye. No, this is praise to God. This is giving God glory for what He has done.

CHAPTER 15

⌇

If You Are Afraid to Give God Glory, It's a Sign that You Are Becoming a Bottom-Feeder

Are you afraid to tell others about your blessings? Or do you find yourself hiding them or making light of what God has given you? When others see what God has done for you, do you dismiss it quietly? Or do you boast on God?

If you shrink back, you are losing a great opportunity to give God the glory He rightly deserves. You are also cutting off the future blessings of others who would be inspired by your testimony to search the Word, act on it, and believe God for blessings in their own life.

God can and will do "whatsoever" you have the pure faith and tenacity to believe Him for, but He commands you to remember where your blessings came from. It's God alone who gives you the power to get wealth so that you can establish His covenant in the earth (Deuteronomy 8:18). So, once you get it, say something! Shout! God's Word works.

You see, it's good to shout for joy and be glad, knowing that God takes pleasure in your prosperity. He knows that you favor His righteous cause and He wants to be magnified in your life (Psalm 35:27). Yes, prosperity is for you to enjoy. Yes, prosperity is for you to bless others. Yes, it's for establishing God's covenant on the earth. But it is also so that you will magnify His holy name. God gets literal pleasure in seeing you blessed. Why would you want to hide what He's done?

Unless He expressly tells you not say something, you should make it a habit to praise God for all He has done and will do for you—the little things, the big things, or whatever you notice at the time when others are around. Let them know what God has done for you. You're not bragging on yourself, you're bragging on the goodness of your God!

FEAR AND PRIDE—THE INTERTWINED ROOT

If telling others is a problem for you, I've found it's usually due to two things: **1) Fear of what others think, or 2) pride that you didn't do it all by yourself.** It could also be a combination of both because those two usually work together. If you let them, this intertwined root will choke your good intentions and steal the good words right out of your mouth. It's the root that will keep you quiet and cut God out of the praise He deserves.

Now, it may *seem* like a form of humility *not* to talk about your blessings. Talking about your blessings might seem like bragging to you and you may wrongly think that it's better not to share what God's done. Maybe you fear a backlash and don't want others to feel uncomfortable or envious, or maybe you just don't want to stand out from the crowd. Those motives aren't godly humility. They are just fear.

Pride looks different. If you say things like, "Well, I'm the one who did this," or "I'm the one who made this happen," well then, you are having a moment of fleshly pride and taking God out of the equation when it comes to your blessings. Yes, you did this and that, but *Who* do you think put air in your lungs so that you could do anything at all? Who do you think gave you that brain? Who gave you that body and that soul? Who recreated your spirit so that you could even know God?

Respect your Father. Give Him the praise He is due because He deserves to hear your praise and others, whether they receive it as good or not, need to hear what He is capable of doing through someone like you.

All of us have people we can reach with news about what God can do. I can't reach everyone. You know people I will never meet or be able to help. And all of us can thank God for something! It doesn't matter how small, we can be thankful. When you hold back praising God for blessings in your life, it's a form of ingratitude. Think of it like that, and it may help you to see that you really are not bragging on yourself but on the goodness of God. The more you see it as gratitude and praise, the more you will have no problem saying, "God has been good to me! Look at what He has done in my life!"

Fear of others can sometimes be hard to overcome. If that's the case, just work on seeing the correlation between your blessings and God's position as the One who gave you the power to gain them. Work on honoring God as your Source in small things. The more you do it, the easier it will get. Work on acknowledging Him to people in your day-to-day life and it will build a good habit that will help you remove the fear of telling others. It will put a stop to any fleshly pride that rises up, too. Because how can you boast in yourself if your focus is on the Lord?

There's Pollution at the Bottom of the Barrel
A Fearful Mind Is a Poor Mind

The business God helped you to grow, the position He gave you, the talents He put in you to hone, the home He helped you to buy, the car He gave you to drive, the food in your fridge and the clothes on your back, if you refuse to give God glory for the tangible things that you know He gave you and the favor He placed on your life to get to the place you are, it's a sign that you are diving low again to the bottom of the barrel.

Pride and fear will turn you into what you were never created to be—a bottom-feeding scavenger content to eat the scraps. God has created you to feast with Him and share what you know with others.

If you let fear or pride come in and rob you of your voice, you'll start short-changing God and yourself in other ways, too. When you should be on top, looking up to Jesus as the Author and Finisher of your faith and enjoying the overflow, you'll find yourself so distracted by the opinions of others that you swim to the bottom of the barrel just to fit in. Do you know what is at the bottom of the barrel? All the junk! The lower you go, the thicker the layers of sediment. Those lowly mindsets that keep people stuck looking down and never going any higher are pollution to your soul. Don't swim back down to a place that God delivered you from. Don't get comfortable with the mental pollution at the bottom of the barrel. Keep your faith in God and what's at the top of the barrel and let your voice of praise be heard for every inch you swam to get to where you are today.

Remember that you can't bring God much glory if you are always hiding what He's done out of fear or pride. But you can bring Him great glory by talking about what He's done, always pointing to Him as the reason behind every blessing!

There's Pressure at the Bottom of the Barrel
A Pressured Mind Is a Poor Mind

Another thing that can sink you to the bottom of the barrel is pressure. The more God blesses you, the more you usually have to take care of—more details, more people, more ideas, and more work, along with more money and possessions. Don't think that you have to be weighted down by the things that come along with being blessed.

Pressure is just one way the devil tries to steal your joy and steal your peace. But the devil is a liar! He's always looking for ways to kill, steal, and destroy God's children (John 10:10). The devil will even try to use God's blessings to push your head under the water and drive you to the bottom of the barrel in your own mind. Don't let him! It's just another tactic to keep you poor when Jesus came to give you a life of abundance.

Once you notice that this is a tactic of the devil, you can deal with it, moving those pressured and anxiety-laced thoughts out and replacing them with the Word of God. Turn Proverbs 10:22 into a personal confession to remind yourself that God's blessings don't come with strings of sorrow. You can say, "The blessing of the Lord makes me rich and He adds no sorrow to the riches!" Sadness and anxiety of any kind is not from God. You can also turn Ecclesiastes 5:18-19 into a personal confession: "God, You are giving me the gift of riches and possessions and the power to enjoy them!"

God gives you the power to enjoy what you have. The devil wants to take that enjoyment away to force you to live in poverty in some way or fashion. Even if God has helped you to earn great riches, even if God has given you incredible favor, and even if you have everything you need or want, the devil will work at stealing your peace of mind. He wants you to live in a place of poverty in your own mind because he knows, as does just about everyone, that a pressured mind is a poor mind!

It doesn't matter how rich you are, if your mind is full of pressure, you cannot enjoy what is in front of you and you can't think very far outside of yourself to help others.

The Bible tells us that God is not the author of confusion (1 Corinthians 14:33). Don't let the devil confuse you. Jesus is the Author and Finisher of our faith (Hebrews 12:2). Notice, He's not like the devil who just starts things and doesn't finish anything. No, Jesus starts and finishes; He can help you with your faith to crush that pressure that Satan tries to use to steal, kill, and destroy your peace of mind. So, go with God! Faith eliminates all confusion.

The Parable of the Sower was a teaching of Jesus that He said applies to everything in the Word. The Sower sows the Word. Are finances in the Word? Yes, they are. So, you can take Mark 4 and apply it to absolutely everything in the Word from witnessing to offerings, from scriptures that you are sowing into your heart to even the pressure and tactics of the devil when it comes to finances. The devil's goal is to lead you off course so that you don't reap the fullness of prosperity.

The "cares of the world" in Mark 4:19 choke the Word. Yielding to anxiety and pressure over your blessings can fall into this category. You can turn Mark 4:19 into a confession and say, "I will never let the cares of this world choke the good Word out of my life. No, I will be fruitful and I will reap in every area—spiritually, mentally, emotionally, and financially!" Don't give the devil an inch in this area.

If God blesses you with something, just know that He has also blessed you with the mind to handle it. You have the mind of Christ and Christ means "Anointed One." Is Christ's mind worrying? Is He under pressure? Is He full of anxiety? No.

You have the anointing to handle whatever blessings come your way, but you will have to put down the thoughts that arise that try and steal your peace. Don't worry! You got this! Don't let the devil lie to you and twist your mind. Don't let him turn your blessing into a curse over the details of dealing with it.

I REFUSE THE POVERTY OF MIND I CALL **PRESSURE!**

I know some of the biggest ministers in this country and I can't tell you how many tell me things like, "Jesse, you're just not under pressure at all. I don't see how you do it." You see, they know what it takes to operate a ministry of this size. They know the pressures that come with it. They know the price of television airtime and all the rest that comes along with a worldwide ministry.

I'm glad when they say it because it helps me to realize that others notice what faith in God can do; that it doesn't just bring you success, but it also settles the soul as you live and work in whatever God has called you to do. So, I share what I believe about pressure and how I get it off of my back. I say things like, "You know, I am not good enough to generate the money it takes to operate this ministry. I know it. I wish I was that good, but I'm not that good. So, I don't even worry about it because I know that this is ALL God's doing. When I get bills, I tell Jesus 'You've got mail!' I cast my cares on the Lord. This is His ministry. As long as I do what I'm supposed to do—be fruitful, multiply, replenish, and subdue what tries to take me off course—He will handle His part. I just have to be a good steward, keep my life clean, and do what I know to do. The whole thing is faith. If I thought it was me, I couldn't do it! I know it's Him, and that alleviates the pressure."

I've been in full-time ministry since 1978. In all that time to the writing of this book, I've never had to lay off an employee. Not one employee has missed a check for the work they've done. Even during Hurricane Katrina, we did everything we could and succeeded at getting our staff their paychecks. That is a miracle of God!

The economy has done all sorts of things over the years, but I've stayed the course and the ministry has not had loss because of the highs and lows of the world. That is a miracle of God, too. I haven't changed my core mission, which is very simple: "Reaching People and Changing Lives, One Soul at a Time." It's that simple. Whatever tries to veer me off course, I put back in line.

I've had many, many offers to do things. I pray about them. Now, if God released me to do them, I would. I am not locked to the plow, so to speak. I'm locked to God's will for my life and this ministry. That's a different thing. I'm going where He goes, not where ego goes. I tell Jesus, "Jesus, if You aren't going with me, I'm not going." I've become very sensitive over the years to His voice and His leading, and I refuse to go off course just because something looks good to the natural eye. You see, I know who I am and I know what God has called me to do; I'm not pretending or playing, I'm doing what God called me to do. This is my purpose and until God tells me otherwise, I will stick with the original plan that He put in my heart over thirty-eight years ago—without the poverty of mind I call PRESSURE!

~

CHAPTER 16

When Light Fades, Darkness Takes Over

Another sign that you are becoming a bottom feeder is when you allow the light of God within you to start to fade. When the light fades, darkness begins to take over. Again, think of Jesus' parable in Mark 14:19. It doesn't just talk about the cares of the world, it also talks about the "deceitfulness of riches" that come in and "choke the Word."

What is the deceit in riches? It's the idea that once you get riches, you don't need God anymore. It's the idea that money itself can be some kind of security when you give money a position in your heart that only God should have: Master.

Money can never become your master. Riches aren't ever supposed to have a place over God in your life.

A tactic of the devil is to try and get you to switch loyalties. It's a tactic to move you to a place of feeling secure enough in your finances that you stop really believing that you need God. This is why it's so hard for an unbeliever who is rich to turn to God and trust Him. They are accustomed to trusting in riches and they don't think they need God because they are taken care of. It's usually not until they either lose their riches or become totally impoverished in some other area of life (health, relationships, lack of peace, addictions, etc.) that they stop seeing money as the only answer and turn to the Lord.

This is the proverbial "camel going through the eye of the needle." In other words, if you are fat with riches and think this is all you need, it takes an amazing shift and shrinking of ego to get you to admit that you need more than just your money and yourself—you need God. It's hard, but it's doable! It may be impossible, with man, but all things are possible with God… even a camel going through the eye of a needle!

This same kind of thinking can creep into the life of a believer, even one who uses faith in God to succeed and become rich. It's very easy for people to get lazy with the Lord once they are full and entire, wanting nothing (James 1:4). It's very easy to start trusting in deceitful riches. But just because financial circumstances aren't dire anymore doesn't mean you don't need the Lord.

Sometimes I've seen that when people get blessed, they begin to let go of God; they take less and less care in developing their relationship with Him. It starts subtly. Again, think of the last portion of Jesus' parable in Mark 4:19 that says "the lusts of other things" chokes the Word.

**When your "love for God" starts losing to your
"lusts of other things," you are headed for trouble.**

This was Solomon's problem. He started out so good, got so blessed, but then let lusts take over and his relationship with God slipped into near non-existence. This means that Solomon traded one master for another.

You can turn Mark 4:19 and Luke 16:13 into personal confessions to keep yourself aware: "I will never let the cares of the world, the deceitfulness of riches, or the lust for other things come in and choke Your Word out of my life—I'll be fruitful and reap! I will never serve money! It will never master me! I will serve the Lord because He is my one and only Master."

DON'T LET THE LIGHT FADE— THERE'S ONLY DARKNESS AT THE BOTTOM

A sign that you are going down to the bottom of the barrel is when the light in your life begins to fade and the darkness begins to take over. When the economy dips and you just immediately accept that you are going to feel the repercussions of it instead of leaning on God as your security and using the Word of God, you are letting the light fade.

When you accept sickness as normal and don't even pray about it or use the Word of God, you are letting the light fade. When you allow every distraction that comes to steal your time and your focus from God, His Word, and your own good destiny in Him, you are letting the light fade.

When you accept that someone you know is beyond hope and don't bother helping them because you think nothing will change with them, you are letting the light fade. When you have an opportunity to do good and decide not to, you are letting the light fade. When you accept whatever "comes down the pipe" in life, so to speak, and don't use the Word to change your thoughts or the situation anymore, you are letting the light fade.

> **Prosperity, good relationships, peace of mind, a healthy body, and the joy of living—none of these or any other good thing from the Lord can take care of itself. Just like you are the receiver of good things, you must maintain what is good if you want it to remain.**

Life is always moving forward. It's never going back and it's never staying in the same place. That means that everything requires upkeep. Maintaining your position at the the top requires the light. You just won't be able to see when things are slipping or when you are going off course if the darkness is seeping in and hindering your vision. Being content and being complacent are two different things. Contentment is good, but complacency dims the light in every good area of your life.

You need light to do the upkeep of your spirit and your soul (mind/will/emotions). It's the only way you really get to the top and it's the only way you stay at the top. How many people have you seen slide all the way back down to the bottom of the barrel? What happened? You could say that they let the light fade and when you let the light fade, the only thing that is going to happen is darkness will encroach.

I am so excited when I see people use their faith in God to reach the top in whatever area they desire. My hope and prayer is that all who believe God and receive His amazing blessings decide to keep God first place. There is no surer way to lose what you gain (in your heart, mind, and sometimes even materially) than to let the light within you fade into darkness.

God's ight in your life must stay valuable to you. He'll help you get to the top. I pray that you always let Him help you to stay there, because the devil is roaming like a lion seeking whom he may devour (1 Peter 5:8). There is nothing sadder than seeing someone gain the world but lose their soul, so to speak. You need a light-filled mind, will, and emotions to get to the top and stay there.

CHAPTER 17

~

If You Stay at the Bottom Too Long, You Begin to Lose Your "Eyes"

God has called us to see with eyes that are enlightened by His Holy Spirit. He is even able to give us insight and vision that will help us ward off the attacks of the enemy in our lives. There is a story in 2 Kings 6:8-20 that talks about eyes. There was a war going on between Israel and Syria, and the prophet Elisha was able to "see" the tactics of Syria against Israel so they could head them off. At one point the Syrian king sent a great army in the middle of the night to capture Elisha; they thought the darkness was enough to give them cover. But darkness is not a cover. All it takes is a little light to illuminate things. Elisha had big light!

When the army came and surrounded the Israeli camp, Elisha's servant was panicked and asked "Alas, my master! What shall we do?" Now, this man was with Elisha, he heard the prophet of God all the time, and he had seen his ability to see into the future. In other words, he was right beside a man who had already proved himself able to "see." But the servant still didn't really have faith.

I love what Elisha did when confronted by panic and fear. First, Elisha spoke the spiritual truth about the situation instead of the natural fact before the man's eyes. *"Do not fear, for those who are with us are more than those who are with them"* (2 Kings 6:16 NKJV). This was a statement meant to inspire faith in the young servant.

Elisha didn't stop there. He took it a step further. 2 Kings 6:17 (NKJV) says, *"And Elisha prayed, and said, 'LORD, I pray, <u>open his eyes that he may see.</u>' Then the LORD opened the eyes of the young man, and he saw. And behold, the mountain was full of horses and chariots of fire all around Elisha"* (emphasis mine).

I love that the prophet spoke faith immediately. And I love that he prayed for the man closest to him, who was shaken by fear, to have his eyes opened so that he too could see something other than just that natural army. When that servant boy's eyes were opened, he saw into the spirit realm. He got an eyeful of the angelic army protecting his master Elisha, and Israel.

You may or may not ever be able to see into the spiritual realm like Elisha the prophet, but you can see with the eyes of faith. You can make sure your eyes aren't clouded by doubt and especially by darkness. It's your job to keep the light lit in your own eyes. You do that by refusing to be a bottom feeder, by focusing on God's Word more than the darkness in this world.

Light can change darkness. The Word and the Holy Spirit illuminate our eyes so that we don't just run around like animals living by instinct, but we become who we were created to be—sons and daughters of God who see clearly and navigate life well.

Every generation of believers is responsible to help the next generation understand and grasp the value of light.

Each generation will be tempted by darkness, that's how the world keeps falling into the same messes of harming each other, disrespecting God, dishonoring His light, and falling into the fleshly depravity that only sees and desires the natural. You talk about bottom feeding? That's it—when people get so depraved that they turn what's good into what's bad and what's bad into what's good.

If we don't train our children to appreciate the light and goodness of God, if we don't tell them how to enjoy life without hurting others, and if we don't show them how to find their own purpose and destiny in God so that they are fulfilled, then we are basically turning down the lights so that they can get accustomed to a bottom feeder's life. And the lower you turn the lights, the darker everything gets.

GENERATIONS BORN WITH NO EYES

If you go down deep into the Atlantic Ocean or deep into the Pacific Ocean, you will find fish with no eyes. They don't need eyes at all because they evolved in the total darkness of the deep sea where there is no light.

Humanity has delved into darkness many times before, forsaking the light for the darkness and reaping the results not only in their lifetimes, but in their children's lifetimes as well. It's called the evolution of darkness. Unless someone shines some light, what else will people do but delve into the layers of darkness?

How many generations of welfare does it take before the children are born with no eyes? How many generations before the children can't see any other way to live? It's a blessing that the government helps the poor because we desperately need that, but today, I see many who are nearly proud they are on welfare. They literally feel like they are getting one over on the government. You see, after a while, the generations just begin to rely on the crutch because they literally don't see a way out. Nobody has shown them a way out. I'm not talking about only a way out of material poverty through education, although of course that's important, but I'm also talking about a way out of the mental poverty that comes when a person literally does not believe they can do it. When their "eyes" are gone, who will help them see?

Where are the spiritually strong fathers and mothers? Where are those spiritually strong grandmothers? Where is family that helps develop a strong spirit in a child? How will people know what they are capable of if they are not shown? And how will they see with smaller and smaller eyes...or no eyes at all? Miracles need to happen! God can do it! He can break all that wrong belief, but we have to start turning the light on so that we can develop eyes to see.

In My Generation, People Didn't Walk into Schools and Kill

We now live in an era where light is no longer equated with God; we have shaken hands with the darkness. We've invited it to sit down in our once brightly-lit rooms, thinking that the darkness would stay put. Darkness never stays put. It moves forward. It encroaches more and more, to whatever degree you will not resist it, and it will take all it can until there is little if no light to be found.

This world has changed. Here in America, more and more godliness is being removed. No mention of the Lord is allowed in most schools. No mention of basic right and wrong takes place without vehement arguments about why darkness is really light. No prayer is mentioned at all, until something goes terribly wrong. Only in tragedy is the Lord or prayer allowed to be spoken without a clampdown of disdain.

In my generation, people never walked into schools with automatic weapons to kill innocent children and teachers. Why? There was more hunting back then than there is today, especially where I grew up in South Louisiana. I had a gun at five years old. There were probably more guns on the market than even today. We had guns! But the people behind those guns were different.

Do you know one reason why people from my generation didn't go into schools and start shooting up the innocent? Because their grandmas and their mamas dragged their little butts to church for years and years, even if they didn't like it. People grew up hearing clear-cut teaching on knowing right from wrong.

I can remember my mother saying, "You're going to church whether you like it or not. You are going to respect people whether you like it or not. You will get up and give a pregnant woman or any women your seat on the bus. You will not talk to your elders with a disrespectful mouth. If you cuss in front of me, you are going to feel my hand across that mouth. And if you raise your hand to me or another woman, I promise you, you may not live another day!"

My mama was Cajun French and talked hard, and I never once considered it threatening. It was more like a prophecy written in advance if I happened to do it! That's a joke, but you get the point.

WHEN SUNDAY WAS FOR CHURCH AND THE FAMILY

Say what you want about the church and its failings, it does preach the value of life and the value of the soul. Anytime that you and your children spend contemplating your soul and others or your life and the importance of humanity is a day well spent. We don't do this anymore.

I remember when Sunday was sacred. They closed the malls on Sunday and no shops but the grocery stores and gas stations were open. Why? It was pointless to open because everybody was in church in the morning and with their family in the afternoon. In fact, they didn't have football on Sundays. Football was on Friday night and Saturdays.

There was a general understanding that it was good for people to have one day a week when they honored God, spent time with their family, and rested from all the buying and selling that went on all week long. That day of rest meant a day to set aside for God—for honoring Him and thanking Him. There are some traditions that we've lost that truly help society, and I believe that is definitely one!

Black Grandmas and Light in the Black Race

I've studied many races, and I think the black race is one of the most phenomenal God ever created. It seems like the capacity this race has to praise God even under the worst of circumstances is off-the-charts full of faith in God.

When they were hanging blacks in Mississippi, when they were burning blacks, destroying their children, and even raping their women, this race (the ones here in America) didn't blame God. They still praised God when they were allowed. They sang "Amazing Grace" and defended God, gave Him credit for any blessing and refused to allow the hatred of others to poison them against God.

I love the black race. I'm Cajun and I might look white, but, really, we don't know what we are. We are just as mixed as they come and I don't care. But today, when I see how things have changed and I see so many people nearly proud to kill, proud to hate, and proud to take something without earning it, it hurts me because my generation saw those black grandmothers washing floors to earn money to send those grandbabies to college.

It's my generation that saw those black grandmas doing everything they knew to do to make a way for their children to succeed. What did my generation have? Eyes to see! Light! There was a lot of light in the blacks of my generation; I mean a bright, white, shining light of God. They knew that poverty was a curse and didn't accept a preacher saying otherwise! You see, if you experience real poverty, you usually have no problem with prosperity in the Bible.

What did those grandmas have? A desire to hold onto the things of God and a desire to see their families have something better, something they didn't mind gaining by work. You didn't see a lot of ego back then, but you did see confidence. There's a difference. You didn't see so much complaining, but you did see a lot of hard work. Proverbs 13:11 tells us that wealth gotten by pure vanity evaporates, but what you gain through labor increases you. Why labor? What does it increase? Character and also, an appreciation for what it takes to increase.

The Family—If We Could See into the Spirit, We'd See the Attacks

I believe that if you could see into the spirit realm and go back in time to *that* time, you would see an army waging war against the light of God in the family. That's right. The family! It's almost as if the devil said, "Let's attack the grandmas! Let's attack those fathers! Take them out! Get rid of the strong fathers and we can break that whole race."

An attack on the family of *any* race is an attack on the light of God, because He instituted the first man and woman and He told them to be fruitful, multiply, replenish, and subdue this earth. Sometimes we have to step back and see into that spirit realm the best way we can. Ask God to open our eyes and the eyes of those working alongside us so that we can see the attacks on our own families and others, and stop the deterioration of the generations.

When a gang is the only family someone knows, no matter what his race or nationality, what can you expect him to do but follow the rules of his "family"? When he shoots an innocent baby or some child or some random person on the street and doesn't feel a thing, there is something wrong with his eyes. He didn't get that way overnight.

In Every Area, Society Is Pushing Further into the Darkness

Disregard for life is now a part of life. You see it in the self-ishness, the egos, the violence, the abuse of children, and the sexual slavery of the young and women that is so common but hidden in the world today. You see it in the senseless murders, the rapes, the entertainment society enjoys. In every area, society is pushing further and further into the darkness.

You even see it in the choices our world has made to "visually" buy and sell its people in pornography, as if human beings are nothing more than a collection of parts—parts to use, wear out, and throw away because there's one more disposable person in line to sell themselves short and one more consumer who wants to buy something new.

Satan is the prince of darkness. I like to say that he's been in the darkness so long, he doesn't have any eyes, so the only eyes he can use are yours and mine. It's good to imagine that the only way he can get you to lust is by using *your* eyes or using *your* body. He has neither. So, if he tries to get you to use your eyes, tell him, "No, these belong to me and I don't want them scraped on the bottom of the barrel, because that's where you're trying to take me."

When you look at the world, you might ask yourself how it got this far. I'll tell you how. It gets dark when a society collectively agrees to dim the lights.

Today, we've dimmed the lights so low that we let darkness have its way. And it's doing what it's always done: Killing, stealing, and destroying people. Do you honestly think there is anything new under the sun when it comes to the devil and sin?

Today, the church doesn't even want to talk about sin. You can't love the devil into repentance; he is beyond that. As unpopular as it sounds, the devil is still working on the earth today to tempt people away from the light and into the darkness of sin and poverty of spirit, mind, and body. Open your eyes! The attack on the light and humanity is spiritual, as it always has been. If we do not turn on the spiritual light, the darkness and the works of the flesh will just get worse on this earth.

That's what happened to the country of Rome when it began to degenerate. Rome was a phenomenal republic at one time. Then it became an empire and it became filled with so much sin that it just destroyed people, and Rome eventually destroyed itself. Darkness invites its own destruction, one less light at a time.

It's tempting to attack people themselves for the problems, but that's not God's way. That's a Christian bottom-of-the-barrel way of dealing with darkness. No, our battle isn't with people themselves, but with the spiritual influence of darkness on the earth. Ephesians 6:12 puts it this way, *"For we wrestle not against flesh and blood, but against principalities, against powers, against the rulers of the darkness of this world, against spiritual wickedness in high places."*

We fight the principalities and powers in the spirit realm that influence people and want to destroy the light of God on this earth. This is called prayer, yes! But I think it's also simply called "letting your light shine."

THE WORLD NEEDS YOU TO SHINE YOUR LIGHT!

Jesus said, *"You are the light of the world. A city set on a hill cannot be hidden. Nor do people light a lamp and put it under a basket, but on a stand, and it gives light to all in the house. In the same way, let your light shine before others, so that they may see your good works and give glory to your Father who is in heaven"* (Matthew 5:14-16).

The light inside of you should produce good works; the believer's life should never be all talk. It's amazing what just a little bit of light can do. One bulb can light a room. Ten can nearly white it out with light!

> **This is one reason why it's so important that Christians believe for and create wealth on the earth—because a light-filled believer with money and a heart for people has the ability to do more to spread light throughout the earth! And don't we desperately need more light?**

That's why I don't like to see Christians hiding their success and living at the bottom of the barrel. God created us to live at the top. We are the head and not the tail! We are above and not beneath! We are called to shine, not to hide what we've got inside us and what we tangibly have as a result of our faith and effort. So boast on the goodness of God! Talk about it! The more you talk about the Light of the world and do good works, the more you show the world that the light still exists. Some people don't believe it. Show them!

We can turn it around. We can create whatever kind of world we want. We can produce a new generation with eyes and high morality, and we'll do it with good words and a good example of just what it means to prosper and be in health, even as our soul prospers (3 John 2). We can do it!

CHAPTER 18

~

Rise Too Quickly Without Mastering Yourself and You Just Might Blow Up Rising to the Top of the Barrel

When the Great Depression of the 1930's hit in America, the people who went through that great time of crisis never let go of the fear of lack. Even though the economy came back and prosperous times came again to America, many could not shake the mentality that it might happen again. They lived in fear. People do this even today. They may not have gone through something like the Great Depression, but you wouldn't know it by how they live.

Years ago in a place called Zephyrhills, Florida, I went to preach a meeting and saw this beautiful, old classic car in the church parking lot. I'll never forget it. Now, I've always liked classic cars and I noticed this one immediately. It was a 1955 Royal Crown Victoria with a hot pink and cream paint job, and it looked like it could have been bought yesterday.

I was wondering who had restored it when I saw an old lady get out of the car. She walked with a cane and everything, and she headed into the church. This was in 1982. At that time, we had messages on cassette tapes at our product table and they were $2 each.

At the end of the service that night, the old lady came up to me as I was walking back to the product table. She was looking at the cassettes and said, "Oh, I love your ministry. I'd like to have some of these tapes, but, oh, they're so expensive."

I felt so bad. I thought, *Oh, Jesus, I am going to bless this sweet little lady.* So, I said, "Well, let me give you some! What would you like?"

She said, "Oh, would you do that for me? Oh, I just can't thank you enough!" So I started picking out some messages and that's when her daughter walked up.

"Mama, what are you doing," she asked.

"Brother Jesse is giving me some tapes," the old lady replied.

Then, the daughter said something that blew my socks off. "Mama! You've got $49 million in liquid cash in a bank plus all kinds of property!"

And this was the old lady's response. "Yeah…but you never know how long it's gonna last!"

Is that crazy? Now, I found out that the car I'd admired was original, not restored, and she had bought it in 1955. It had something like 7,000 miles on it. You see, she actually had a top of the barrel experience—she was at the top financially—but she was *living* on the bottom.

LIVING AT THE BOTTOM

In 1968, I was a bank teller at Terrebonne Bank & Trust in Houma, Louisiana. I had that job for about three months before I moved on to something else. I remember working one day when a lady came up to the counter with her little passbook savings account. This was a booklet that had the financial information about the account written in it.

"Oh, I hate to withdraw some money out of my account, but I've just got to," she said. "I've got to buy some things." She really seemed to be struggling about whether she would take money out or not. I waited and finally she handed me her booklet and said, "Oh, I just hate to spend fifty dollars."

I opened it and saw that there was $12,680,000 in the passbook. I looked at her and said, "Ma'am, why are you worried about $50?"

She gave me the same answer the old lady with the classic car would give me fourteen years later. "You never know how long it's gonna last," she said. I found out that she was living on a houseboat with no electricity. South Louisiana is a humid and very hot place in the summer. It's sometimes exactly the same at Christmas! So, to live that way when you don't have to is truly a dedicated choice to live at the bottom of the barrel.

What causes a person to do this? In most instances, when I've encountered a person who chooses to live this way when they don't have to, they have one singular issue. Their money has become their security and their "God."

Beware that money does not become your security and your "God." You see, that's called "the love of money." It happens when you fall in love with money and make it the principle thing in your life, as if it is the only thing that can save you. *"For the love of money is the root of all evil: which while some coveted after, they have erred from the faith, and pierced themselves through with many sorrows"* (1 Timothy 6:10).

Money itself isn't bad, but the *love* of money will cause you to err from the faith, and what is the opposite of faith? Fear. The love of money will cut the joy right out of your life. Notice the Word says you'll pierce *yourself* through with many sorrows. It's like throwing away joy with both hands.

Money should never take the place of God in your life; it can't possibly give you true security. Another depression could hit tomorrow and everything become worthless. So your security and joy can't be in something that fleeting. The One who sustains you needs to be God—not the bank!

So, beware of loving money because all that is going to do is make you covet and wish you had more. The love of money will pull you from your faith and push you right into fear. The love of money will pierce you with many sorrows. Let money be money. Let God be God. Reserve your love for God and for people alone, not money!

Avoid Blowing Up Rising to the Top of the Barrel!

Keeping your eyes on God and learning to master yourself is essential as you rise to the top. If you go too fast and ignore those things, you just might blow up on your way to the top of the barrel! You see, the pressure of growth happens fast sometimes, and people who don't work on being successful from the inside out sometimes end up making self-destructive and foolish mistakes that rip success right out of their hands.

They lose what they worked for or lose themselves because they neglected their spirit and never could find the desire to master themselves.

That's why you see some successful people lose it all over personal weaknesses. You look at them and think, *Why can't they just be happy? If I was in their shoes, I would be so happy and thankful. I can't believe they are acting like that! I can't believe they are throwing it away like that!* They may have succeeded in one way, but they rose too fast and neglected to master themselves along the way and the success ended up doing them more harm than good.

Self-control or "temperance" is a fruit of the Spirit of God and if you don't have it, you'll make a mess out of what could be a joyful and stable life. It's required at every moment, all through the range of your personal habits and throughout the course of your life. Be a top feeder who is dominant in spirit, holding his flesh with habitual iron control. It'll help you keep your wits about you as you rise to the top of the barrel.

If You Don't Have Character, You'll Become a Character!

It's said that character is how you act when no one is watching. Well, that's true, but it's also true that your character can be seen when everybody's watching! One of the pitfalls of success is falling into the mindset that your success actually defines who you are and that those who aren't as successful are somehow "less." Boy, is that a trap!

It's a wonderful blessing to live in something nice, to drive something nice, to even fly something nice, and wear something nice. To not have limitations on what you can and cannot buy is a blessing! But you should never define yourself merely by the money, possessions, or success you have believed God for and earned. You should be defined by the character you have. If you don't have character, you will *become* a character!

How can you tell if success or things are defining you in your own mind? You can tell it's happening if you look down on people who have less than you. In Proverbs 6:17-19, the Word tells us seven things that God *hates*—the first one on the list is "a proud look." Some translations use the word "haughty." It's called looking down your nose at others. God hates this, so you should, too. It's ungodly pride and shows bad character. A believer with good character treats people well no matter what their economic status!

Learn to Value Self-Control as Much as the Goal

You see, self-control is a mark of the Holy Spirit. Godly success doesn't come by throwing caution to the wind and doing whatever your flesh dictates. You maintain the right order within yourself by putting your spirit above your soul, and your soul above your body.

The world thinks the other way around—they put the body first, the soul second, and barely consider the spirit. They think "freedom" is consuming everything they see, squandering as much as they can, and polluting themselves with everything mentally and physically that they can manage. That's not freedom. It's just lasciviousness and lack of self-control. Even some believers act this way. Let me give you some insight: living like that leads to a bottom-dwelling life, no matter how much money you've got in the bank. So hold your flesh in check because you value something else greater. It applies to everything natural.

If you don't like your weight and you want to live at the top when it comes to your physical body, you need to value self-control just as much or even more than you value the idealized version of your body that's in your head.

If you want to get out of debt, you need to value self-control just as much or even more than you value the desire to be free of debts and owe no man anything but love. Self-control has to be just as much a part of the dream as the desire to never pay interest again!

If you can't master yourself, you probably won't master anything else. It's got to start with you and that inner desire to put the flesh down and master yourself for the sake of a greater cause and a greater goal.

You have great power. You have free will and the ability to say "yes" or "no." If you desire to master yourself and go to the top in that area, the Holy Spirit within you will help you if you turn to Him in times when you are tempted to give in to a bottom feeder's life. I'm not saying it's fun, but think of it this way: you are still breathing the same 24/7 whether you live low or aim high! So you might as well go for it because increasing self-control and learning to master yourself can really help to propel you to the top. God is looking for people He can use who have mastered themselves enough to lead the way for others.

GOD OFTEN WANTS TO DO MORE WITH LESS JUST TO SHOW YOU THAT HE CAN

In Judges chapter seven, Gideon was leading a battle against the Midianites. You would think that more is better when it comes to how many men were there to fight for Israel. God didn't think so.

Gideon had about 32,000 men. Now, I'm paraphrasing and just focusing on the point of the story that I want to share with you, but basically God told Gideon, "You've got too many men. I'm not going to deliver the other side to that many. I don't want you to think that it was the amount of men that saved Israel. I want you to know that it was because of Me, and Me alone" (my paraphrase, Judges 7:2).

God told Gideon, "The first thing I want you to do is ask who is scared to fight, and whoever says they are, let them go" (my paraphrase, Judges 7:3). So, Gideon did that and 22,000 men left! Only 10,000 remained. Still, that was too many to God.

God said, "I'm going to test them for you. Send the 10,000 down to the water to drink. The ones who get on their knees to drink and the ones who lap up the water like a dog, let those go. But, the ones who bring the water up and lap it from their *hands*, those and only those do I want you to take for the battle" (my paraphrase, Judges 7:4-7).

Now, these must have been some thirsty men because all of them except for 300 men were down on their knees and drinking face-first like dogs. Why God chose this method to choose who would fight was up to Him, but maybe there was something top feeder about the men who wouldn't succumb to looking like dogs by the riverside, even when they were thirsty. There was something, perhaps bottom feeding, about the ones who could care less how they acted the moment they got thirsty.

The point is that Gideon listened. He had faith in God, and God got the men He wanted for the job—300 men with dignity who would still fight even if they were small in numbers, and who would do whatever their leader said to make it happen.

"Then the LORD said to Gideon, 'By the three hundred men who lapped I will save you, and deliver the Midianites into your hand"

(Judges 7:7, njkv). Guess what? Gideon and his 300 valiant men won the battle and nobody could take credit for it because the Scripture says the Lord turned the enemy one against the other and they ended up fleeing the small army.

You see, sometimes 300 men may not make much sense, but when you have 300 top feeders who have faith in God and are following a man who does what God says, God gets involved and they accomplish much more than than 31,700 bottom feeders! Go and read the full story for yourself and you'll see, it was amazing!

CHAMPIONS AT HEART— THEY ALWAYS GIVE IT THEIR BEST

Champions always give their best. I like boxing and one of my favorite fights of all time was between Muhammed Ali and Joe Frazier. They were perfectly matched and it was a miracle they didn't die in that ring, they fought so hard. Ali won, but his respect for Frazier came out when he said, the only difference between them really was that he "lasted two seconds longer." Those men were both champion fighters, and they fought that way. That's what top feeders do!

It's said that the great Italian opera singer from the 1900s, Enrico Caruso, was invited to sing at a small reception. Instead of giving a small performance, he sang as if he was at the Metropolitan Opera. People were just crying, listening and experiencing his huge talent in such a small space. When the manager said, "Enrico, you don't have to sing that hard," he looked at him and said something I find so funny: "That's why you're a manager and I'm the star." He said, "When I sing, I sing my best all the time." That's what top feeders do!

Do you remember how many spies went out to spy the land for the nation of Israel? Twelve. Do you remember how many came back with a good report? Two. Do you remember the names of the ten who came back with a bad report? No. Do you remember the names the two who came back with a good report? Of course you do—everybody talks about Joshua and Caleb when they share on that biblical story. Why? Because people remember top feeders. They remember people who are champions at heart.

God has called each of us to be a champion at heart, not to lap like dogs, not to fight half-heartedly, not to sing with zero passion. No, God has called each of us to follow our divine destiny and to give it all we've got along the way, showing the world that God has anointed us to do what only we can really do. We bring God glory when we aim for the top of the barrel!

CHAPTER 19

No Matter How High You Go, Remember Where You Came From

A while back I was going to eat lunch with a pastor friend of mine and he said, "Jesse, I've got to stop by the house of one of my members. Are you OK with that?"

I said, "Sure, of course."

He said, "Just wait in the car. I won't be long, and then we'll go on to lunch."

I said, "OK."

Now, I came from nothing. I make the joke that I grew up 'po, and that's when you don't even have the money for the last two letters in the word! But, God has blessed me. I can say, like Abraham, that God has made me rich. He's given me favor. He's brought blessings into my life that utterly astound me, and I don't mean that pridefully at all. It's just the truth that God has blessed me and brought me to the top of the barrel.

As he drove up, I noticed that we were going to a mobile home, a trailer that had a little room built onto it. I sat in the car staring and, all of a sudden, I thought, *Wow, that's my mama. That's my daddy. They lived in a trailer just like that until I finally was able to buy them a nice home.*

Well, I got out of that car. I couldn't stop myself from walking right through the little cyclone gate and up to the front door. I knocked on the door and the pastor said, "Oh, Brother Jesse, I apologize. Was I taking too long?"

I couldn't even answer him. I looked inside and saw an old couple. She must have been 78 and he must have been 80 years old. I said, "Hello" and they said, "Oh! Brother Jesse! Would you like to come in?"

"I'd love to come in!" I said, and the pastor told them, "Well, we're going to be leaving in a few seconds."

Now, there was no way I was going anywhere anytime soon. I looked at them and asked, "Y'all got anything to eat?" They smiled and the lady said, "Oh, yeah! We've always got something to eat."

I felt at home. It was like I remember when I went to my grandma's house. All of them are now in Heaven. I looked around the little trailer and you could eat off the floor, it was so clean. It reminded me of my mama. Her floors were so clean that bugs couldn't walk on them without sliding right off!

I noticed two little pots on the stove. It was just the two of them and she hadn't made a lot, but they'd already eaten and that was what was left. She said, "You want a little taste?" That meant she would give me a little spoonful straight from the pot.

I said, "Yeah, yeah, let me have that."

I looked over and I saw a cold, cold bucket of water with a dipper. That struck me because that's going way back, further than most will remember. A dipper! You didn't take water out and put it in glass each time you were thirsty, you pulled up the metal dipper and drank from it and the metal itself seemed to make the water colder.

Well, a taste was not enough and that lady served me. It tasted so good that I asked for more! I wanted more of the petite peas with luncheon meat, something just like I would have eaten growing up.

By this time, the pastor was getting antsy. He had business to do right after our lunch, so I said, "Go ahead, go do your business. I'm gonna stay here and you can pick me up later for tonight's service." So I finished eating and I talked with the couple for a while, and then I got even bolder! I said, "You got a bedroom where I can take a nap?"

She said, "Oh, yes, I do!"

I stayed there the whole afternoon. I took a nap. I'd never met these people before in my life, but it was wonderful! I was raised just like they were living and I have to tell you, I enjoyed myself being with them. I said, "I hope I didn't overstep."

"Oh, no, you sweet little thing, you! Not you," she said. "You come here anytime you want."

I said, "Uh, I will!"

Watching that couple was like watching my parents or my grandparents. He'd sit there and a little something would come out of his mouth and his wife would be walking by and she'd just wipe his mouth as if he was a toddler, you know. Oh, he'd just sit there and take it, and smile a little. If she saw a hair out of place on him, she'd lick her finger and stick the piece back in its place. As you get older, the women just take over. The men ain't got a chance!

Well, life got busy, as usual, and those people passed away about a year and a half ago, at the time of the writing of this book. Later, the pastor would tell me that I made their day and that they talked about my visit all the time. To them, I was famous. To me, they felt like family. The pastor said that when people would come over and visit, they'd say, "Do you know who slept in my house? Do you know who stopped by?"

It was a wonderful day for me to spend time with that couple in that trailer. When I got back to my hotel that night, I prayed to the Lord and He spoke to my heart.

"Enjoyed your day, didn't you?"

I said, "Yeah."

He said, "I appreciated that. You made their day."

I said, "No, Lord, they made my day."

Treasure the Good Things No Matter What

I told you that story to make this point: Being with those people in that trailer was a top of the barrel experience for me. It doesn't matter how I live now, I can't forget where I come from or where I've been along the way in this journey up the barrel. I treasure all the good things from the bottom to the top, because each level in my life has had its own priceless moments. I refuse to resent the journey.

A lot of people, when they rise up and become successful, really loathe the small beginnings. They resent where they came from and say, "I'm never going back to that!" They start looking down their noses at where they came from, as if they were always successful. Some will flat refuse to do anything at all that reminds them of their days at the bottom of the barrel. I think this is a grave mistake.

There are top of the barrel *experiences* and top of the barrel *people* throughout the whole barrel. That day for me had nothing to do with accomplishing a new goal or acquiring a new thing. It had everything to do with experiencing happiness and peace. There was a pure absence of anxiety in that home. It reminded me of moments in my childhood that were good. Although my bottom of the barrel childhood surely wasn't all good and there are things I'd like to forget, the truth is that there were peaceful and happy moments, too.

If the people were good enough for you *before* you had money, what makes them bad people now that you have money? Think about it. No matter how high you go, no matter how far you rise, don't forget where you came from. One day it just might be that the experience of "going back" is one of your greatest moments ever.

May You Enjoy the Ride to the Top and When You Pass, May You Keep Going Straight UP!

Jesus Christ left Heaven to make this earth His home because He thought it was worth it. He came because we were in dire need of saving and because lack had taken hold in every single area of mankind's existence. The message of the Gospel is one of no lack. It takes us from a destitute and impoverished spirit and washes us clean of the sin nature that the Word says is the reason for all the problems in the world that we see and have ever experienced. Jesus and His sacrifice on the cross removes the barrier between man and God and all we have to do to have a new, recreated spirit is to call on His name, accept Him, and begin to really "live" instead of just survive.

When Jesus said He came so that we might have life and that more abundantly, He was talking to all of us—that includes you and that includes me. No matter where we come from or what we have or don't have, He is able to help us rise up and go higher than we ever could on our own.

I might have been born poor, but the Lord has made me rich—I was rich the moment I said, "Jesus, come into my life." I just didn't know it yet. I didn't know how far He would bring me. At that moment, I was a young man who had already made a lot of money playing music. I had everything financially that I wanted, but I was still living at the bottom in life. I was scraping the barrel thinking that I was free.

When Jesus came into my life, I saw the greatness of lack in my life. He alone picked me up, loved me anyway, and began to show me, through His Word and books like this one and messages from good men of God, that I could have a life worth something. Not just "success" as the world sees it, but something bigger and purer than I ever imagined possible.

That's what I'm believing He will do for you too. No matter if you've been saved one minute or fifty years, God can take you higher in this life. Don't be afraid to dream and use your faith for big things. He can heal your mind, your emotions, and even your body. He can teach you how to really live and handle what comes your way. He can help you to say "no" to the things that won't bring you anywhere but to the bottom, and "yes" to the things that will help you rise above it all and live at the top.

My prayer for you is the Lord's Prayer. I'd like to end this book with that now because Jesus prayed something here that very few people really grasp. I'll bold it so that you can see what I'm believing for you.

*"Our Father which art in heaven, Hallowed be thy name. Thy kingdom come. **Thy will be done in earth, as it is in heaven**. Give us this day our daily bread. And forgive us our debts, as we forgive our debtors. And lead us*

not into temptation, but deliver us from evil: For thine is the kingdom, and the power, and the glory, for ever. Amen."

Matthew 6:9-13

It was Christ's prayer that you would know and live the Father's will—that God's will would be done right here on earth as it is in Heaven. Is there any lack in Heaven? In any area whatsoever that is good, is there any lack? I pray that you rise up and find your own personal place at the top of the barrel; a place where everything you touch prospers and every area you put your faith towards explodes with the abundant nature of Heaven.

May you enjoy the ride and have the time of your life. And one day, when you pass over to that other side, I pray that you keep on going straight up, all the way to Heaven! I hope that when you get there, you find that it is a whole lot like the life you created with God and lived right here on earth fulfilled with all the best things—spiritual, physical, financial and in every other way!

God bless you as you seek Him and act in faith on His Word. I know that you're going to end up exactly where you want to be and where He has always planned for you to live—at the TOP!

Prayer of Salvation

"For God so loved the world, that he gave his only begotten Son, that whosoever believeth in him should not perish, but have everlasting life. For God sent not his Son into the world to condemn the world; but that the world through him might be saved."

John 3:16-17

God loves the world. He sent His Son, Jesus, to make a way for all of us to be free—from guilt, from shame, and from every sin and misstep no matter how big or small. Salvation removes the heavy chains of sin and a life lived apart from our Maker. Christ's death and resurrection on the cross was sacrificial—He did it for you and for me, and for the whole world, so that we could have that blank slate and simply start again.

Accepting God's plan of salvation through Jesus Christ is the first step to living at the top because, as Mark 8:36 says, *"For what shall it profit a man, if he shall gain the whole world, and lose his own soul?"* Nothing is as important as being right with God in your heart and, by accepting Christ, you are doing just that.

If you don't know my Jesus today, if you've never prayed a prayer of salvation or if you just need to come back home to God where you belong, would you take a moment and pray with me today? This prayer below is a guide. Feel free to talk from your heart. Wherever you are right now, no matter what your situation, God will meet you where you are—He will hear your prayer, loose the chains of bondage off of your soul, and set you free with the blood of His precious Son, Jesus. Pray with me now:

"God, thank You for loving me enough to send Your Son. I know that I need You. I believe that You are my God, my Maker, and my Father—and I believe that You sent Your only begotten Son to die for me. I believe that He died and rose again for me, too, so that I could be washed clean of all my sins. Jesus, come into my life right now. Wash me clean and create a new heart in me now. Thank You for paying the price for me. From this point on, I will seek to serve You and love You, and I ask You to help me to find my destiny in You—to be whole in every area of my life. May Your blessings follow me all the days of my life as I learn from You. Thank You, Jesus, for saving me! My new life starts right now, Lord. This is my God-day and I'm never turning back!"

If you have prayed this prayer or if this book has helped you to create a good life in Christ, would you write and let me know? Please write to:

Jesse Duplantis Ministries
PO Box 1089
Destrehan, LA 70047-1089
www.jdm.org

Salvation Confessions

If you just prayed the salvation prayer or you'd like to remind yourself of what God has already done for you, I encourage you to use the following confessions and scriptures to determine and affirm your decision to follow Christ. God bless you as you live for God and carve out your BEST life in Him!

Today is the day of salvation. 2 Corinthians 6:2 – *"Behold, now is the accepted time; behold, now is the day of salvation."*

God sent His Son to save me. John 3:16-17, *"For God so loved the world that he gave his only begotten Son, that whoever believes in him should not perish but have everlasting life. For God did not send his Son into the world to condemn the world, but that the world through him might be saved."*

Like all, I've sinned and fallen short, but grace is provided through Jesus. Romans 3:23-24 – *"For all have sinned, and come short of the glory of God; being justified freely by his grace through the redemption that is in Christ Jesus."*

Jesus is patient and loving. 2 Peter 3:9 – *"The Lord is not slack concerning His promise, as some count slackness, but is long-suffering toward us, not willing that any should perish but that all should come to repentance."*

I believe in my heart that Jesus resurrected, I confess with my mouth that He is my Lord – I am saved by faith in God's Word. Romans 10:9-10 – *"If you confess with your mouth* the Lord Jesus and believe in your heart that God has raised Him from the dead, you will be saved. For with the heart one believes unto righteousness, and with the mouth confession is made unto salvation" (NKJV).

I call on the name of the Lord knowing He will save me. Acts 2:21 – "And it shall come to pass that whoever calls on the name of the LORD shall be saved" (NKJV).

I am not ashamed of what Christ did for me, I live by faith now! Romans 1:16-17 – "For I am not ashamed of the gospel of Christ, for it is the power of God to salvation for everyone who believes, for the Jew first and also for the Greek. For in it the righteousness of God is revealed from faith to faith; as it is written, 'The just shall live by faith'" (NKJV).

He loved me while I was still a sinner, He saved me from His wrath. Romans 5:8-9 – "But God demonstrates His own love toward us, in that while we were still sinners, Christ died for us. Much more then, having now been justified by His blood, we shall be saved from wrath through Him" (NKJV).

I am new creation in Christ! 2 Corinthians 5:17 – "Therefore, if anyone is in Christ, he is a new creation; old things have passed away; behold, all things have become new" (NKJV).

I am delivered from darkness and forgiven of all my sin! Colossians 1:13-14 – "He has delivered us from the power of darkness and conveyed us into the kingdom of the Son of His love, in whom we have redemption through His blood, the forgiveness of sins" (NKJV).

I am redeemed, I'm abounding in His grace. Ephesians 1:7-8 – *"In Him we have redemption through His blood, the forgiveness of sins, according to the riches of His grace which He made to abound toward us in all wisdom and prudence"* (NKJV).

I didn't earn my salvation, but I'm assured of it because I have faith and I serve a God of mercy and grace. Ephesians 2:8-9 – *"For by grace you have been saved through faith, and that not of yourselves; it is the gift of God, not of works, lest anyone should boast"* (NKJV).

So, I will confess Jesus before others knowing Jesus will confess me before God! Matthew 10:32 – *"Whosoever therefore shall confess me before men, him will I confess also before my Father which is in heaven."*

I will not draw back, I will live by faith and believe! Hebrews 10:38-39 – *"Now the just shall live by faith: but if any man draw back, my soul shall have no pleasure in him. But we are not of them who draw back unto perdition; but of them that believe to the saving of the soul."*

With Christ, I have strength and can do all things! Philippians 4:13 – *"I can do all things through Christ which strengtheneth me."*

About the Author

Jesse Duplantis is what some would call a true evangelist. Supernaturally saved and delivered from a life of addiction in 1974 and called by God to the office of evangelist in 1978, he founded Jesse Duplantis Ministries with the sole mission of world evangelism at whatever the cost. And he has continuously done that for almost four decades of ministry work.

With a television ministry that spans the globe, ministry offices is America, the United Kingdom, and Australia, and a preaching itinerary that has taken him to thousands of different churches to date, Jesse is still fulfilling his original call to evangelism with gusto! His commitment to Christ, long-standing integrity in ministry, and infectious, joyful nature have made him one of the most loved and respected ministers of the Gospel today.

Often called the "Apostle of Joy" because of his hilarious illustrations, Jesse's anointed preaching and down-to-earth style have helped to open the door for countless numbers of people to receive Jesus as their Lord and Savior. Jesse has proven through his own life that no matter who you are or where you came from, God can change your heart, develop your character through His Word, and help you find and complete your divine destiny.

Jesse Duplantis Ministries has one goal: to share God's message of salvation through Jesus Christ with the world. We want everyone to have an opportunity to know the real Jesus. Approachable, personable, compassionate, and full of joy, that's the real Jesus that Jesse Duplantis knows and loves. And it's his mission in life to make sure everyone on every continent has an opportunity to know Jesus, too.

Jesse Duplantis Ministries is making a difference. Through worldwide television broadcasting, ministry resources such as DVDs, CDs, and digital media, Christian literature including books and our monthly magazine, internet and social media outreaches, and meetings held around the globe, Jesse Duplantis Ministries is "reaching people and changing lives, one soul at a time." Jesse Duplantis is reaching out with the Gospel in a way that is captivating the lost and turning hardened hearts back to their first love. People are responding to this joyful, down-to-earth, and passionate ministry. They're tuning in. They're listening and laughing. Most of all, they're realizing the freedom, simplicity, and joy that comes from being at peace with God and in love with His Son, Jesus.

At JDM, we're committed to keeping our focus unclut-tered—pure and simple, just like Christianity is supposed to be. We're proud to have one vision, one goal, one mission: World Evangelism. It's our passion! And we invite you to join with us and make it your passion, too.